CHURCHES IN NORTH AMERICA
An Introduction

CHURCHES
IN
NORTH AMERICA

An Introduction

By Gustave Weigel, S.J.

HELICON PRESS
Baltimore

Library of Congress Catalog Card Number 61–17627

The chapters of this book originally appeared as articles in *Hi-Time*, published by Hi-Time Publishers, Inc., Milwaukee, Wisconsin. The author is very grateful to Hi-Time Publishers for permission to collect the articles into book form.

Copyright © 1961 by Helicon Press, Inc.
All Rights Reserved

Nihil Obstat: EDWARD A. CERNY, S.S., S.T.D.
Censor Librorum

Imprimatur: ✠ FRANCIS P. KEOUGH, D.D.
Archbishop of Baltimore
October 13, 1961

The *Nihil Obstat* and *Imprimatur* are official declarations that a book or pamphlet is free of doctrinal or moral error. No implication is contained therein that those who have granted the *Nihil Obstat* and *Imprimatur* agree with the opinions expressed.

PRINTED IN THE UNITED STATES OF AMERICA BY THE NORTH CENTRAL PUBLISHING COMPANY, SAINT PAUL, MINNESOTA

PREFACE

Distinct fellowships of Christians have proliferated greatly in our Western society since the sixteenth century. We have become accustomed to use the word *churches* to describe the various organized unions of local congregations. When these different (and sometimes even hostile) churches share somehow in a particular vision of Christian faith and life derived from some past churchman or historical church group, we have come to refer to them as *denominations*. There are today more than two hundred and fifty churches in the United States alone, and they are described in many books.

But quite recently there has been a counter-tendency among the many churches and denominations. New combinations, all moving toward unity, are appearing. A developing awareness of Christians as the Body of Christ which is the Church seems to be a basic impulse here. And Catholics, as evidenced by discussions of the coming ecumenical council, are becoming more and more sympathetically aware of this. A greater desire to know and understand the bewildering variety of fellow Christians is growing. This group of sketches of the pluralism of American church life (originally published in a Catholic secondary school journal) is an attempt to describe briefly many, but not all, of our churches.

The task is a challenge. A combination of simplicity, accuracy and a friendly approach to the religious bodies described is required. The reader I have in mind is the man or woman who wants a brief description of the many churches in our commonwealth so that he or she may know in a schematic fashion what the churches stand for and how they collectively exercise their piety.   4 5 2 59

Members of a given church here described may be somewhat dissatisfied because so little is said about something well known and dear to them. This reaction I cannot avoid if I wish to pursue the goal of brevity. Other readers will be amazed that their church is not even mentioned. But I could not do them all. Yet I do hope that each group will find in these sketches the friendliness and good will I have for them, even though my understanding is defective. Catholics will be surprised that their church is not included, but the book is written for them primarily. I can therefore presume that they need no thumbnail sketch of it.

It was stated above that there are other books which give descriptions of the American churches of our time. It might be useful for the reader to know them.

Each year DR. BENSON Y. LANDIS edits the *Yearbook of American Churches*, which is published by the National Council of Churches, New York. Brief descriptions of all the churches are there given along with the latest statistics available.

FRANK S. MEAD. *Handbook of Denominations in the United States*. New York & Nashville: Abingdon, 1951.

ELMER T. CLARK. *The Small Sects in America*. Rev. ed. New York & Nashville: Abingdon, 1949.

VERGILIUS FERM, (ed.). *The American Church of the Protestant Heritage*. New York: Philosophical Library, 1953.

———— (ed.). *Religion in the Twentieth Century*. New York: Philosophical Library, 1948.

F. E. MAYER. *The Religious Bodies of America*. St. Louis: Concordia Publishing House, 1954.

J. PAUL WILLIAMS. *What Americans Believe and How They Worship*. New York: Harper & Brothers, 1952.

Two Catholic authors have also published books of the same kind.

JOHN A. HARDON, S.J. *The Protestant Churches of America*. Westminster, Maryland: Newman, 1958.

WILLIAM J. WHALEN. *Separated Brethren. A Survey of non-Catholic Christian Denominations in the United States*. Milwaukee: Bruce, 1958.

G. Weigel, S.J.

CONTENTS

CHURCHES IN NORTH AMERICA
An Introduction

1. THE ONE CHURCH AND THE MANY CHURCHES

Jesus of Nazareth lived and died something less than 2000 years ago. His followers came to think of themselves as Christ's Church; and by Christ's teaching that Church must be one, even as he and the Father are one. Church unity was urged by Jesus on his disciples. It was to be taken as the sign which showed that they were truly Christian.

Yet in spite of this great stress Jesus gave to the oneness of his Church, Christian history from the earliest days showed divisions which were bitter and saddening. In the pages of the New Testament we find described two classes of Christians which were not accepted by the Church universal. In the second epistle of St. John (v. 10–11), the members of the Apostolic Church were told to have nothing to do with a man whose beliefs were not derived from the Apostles: "Do not receive him into the house, or say to him, Welcome. For he who says to him, Welcome, is sharer in his evil works."

The two groups which worried the infant Church were the Judaizers and the Gnostics. The Judaizers were Jewish Christians who considered Christianity to be a way of following Jewish religion. They demanded that all Christians, even those who had not been Jews before their conversion, should observe Jewish customs and Jewish fellowship. St. Paul fought these ideas and showed that Christianity was a new religion to which the older Jewish faith had pointed, but had not achieved. The Judaizers did not outlive the first century of our era.

The Gnostics, however, were quite different. The word *Gnostic* means a man who has knowledge, who knows the deeper truth. The Gnostics accepted the teachings of the Apostles but promptly interpreted them in a way alien to Apostolic intent. They followed philosophic notions drawn

3

from the East and dressed up in the philosophic language of the Greeks. As a formal sect, they finally died out in the fifth century.

At no moment of the history of the Church do we find an unbroken union among all those who called themselves Christians. There were both large secessionist groups like the Arians and little sects like the Donatists. As against all these separatists the Church from the fourth century onwards called herself Catholic. The continuing, surviving Church was the Catholic Church. Some of the churches outside of the unity of the Catholic Church lived and flourished for hundreds of years, some even to our day. But the others in time wither away and disappear.

It is very interesting to read about and study the divisions within Christianity in ages gone by. However, the divisions of our own times arouse our curiosity more. They should, because they affect our own lives here and now. In our day there are about 300 different Christian churches. Some are very small and exist in narrow geographical boundaries. Others are very large and can be found in many places. Only one is called by the world at large the *Catholic Church* although many other churches include the word "Catholic" in their official titles. But men in general do not call them by this name.

We shall look at the churches other than the one called the Catholic Church (or *Roman Catholic Church* because its center is the Church in Rome under the definitive direction of the Bishop of Rome, commonly called the Pope). These other churches can be grouped around moments of crisis in the history of the Catholic Church. Since we are going to look at the many churches of our own time, we can ignore churches which once existed but today are no more. We need only mention such churches of the past: the Arians, the Montanists, the Donatists, the Albigensians and the Lollards.

But we have with us still some churches which were formed in the 400s of our era. There were two famous councils of the Church in that century. One was the Council of Ephesus in 431 and the other was the Council of Chalcedon in 451.

The One Church and the Many Churches

Many Christians of Syria, Mesopotamia and Persia would not accept the authority of the Council of Ephesus and they formed what is usually called the Nestorian Church, though they today call themselves the *Church of the East and of the Assyrians.* This was once a very numerous and powerful church but today it is dying, numbering less than 75,000 members. Some can be found in the United States and the head of the Church, Mar Eshai Shimun XXIII, lives in California.

After the Council of Chalcedon different groups broke away from unity with the Catholic Church. These churches are usually called Monophysite (i.e. one nature) because they rejected the Council of Chalcedon which taught that in Christ there were two natures, one divine and one human. In reality, this name does not fit these churches because though they reject the Council, they all believe in the two natures of Christ. It is better to call them by the historical names adopted by these churches where they flourished. There are four such churches. The first is the *Coptic Church,* made up of Egyptians whose church worship is conducted in the old Egyptian rite and language. The *Ethiopian Church* in Abyssinia had been organized by the Egyptian Church and followed it in its separation from the Catholic Church. The third non-Chalcedonian church is usually called the *Jacobite Church,* whose 70,000 members for the most part live in Syria, Iraq and Lebanon. This church calls itself the *Syrian Orthodox Church* but must not be confused with the Byzantine Orthodox Church of the same name. The Jacobite Church also has a branch of its followers in India where they are called *Malankarese Christians.* The last of the non-Chalcedonian churches is the *Armenian Gregorian Church* (distinct from the *Armenian Church* in union with Rome), sometimes called the Armenian Orthodox Church, though not at all related to the Byzantine Orthodox churches. Its homeland is in ancient Armenia in Asia Minor, but today it is only found in Georgia, Russia. Many of the Armenians are scattered all over the globe and they carry this church with them. The total membership would amount to three millions, of whom 125,000 live in the United States.

5

CHURCHES IN NORTH AMERICA

The unhappy event which produced a great division in Christianity was the schism between Western Catholics and Eastern Catholics in 1054. From that point on the westerners kept the name *Catholic* and the easterners called themselves *Orthodox*. Eastern Orthodoxy is a sisterhood of many churches comprising 130,000,000 members living for the most part in the European Slav countries and in the Greek-speaking lands of the Mediterranean. Over 3,000,000 of them reside in the United States and we shall speak of them in our next chapter.

In the sixteenth century a great upheaval took place in western Catholicism. Four different threads of opposition to the Catholic Church came out of this movement which is usually called the Protestant Reformation. These four different threads produced new churches which have continued to our time. From these new churches other churches were formed so that today there are at least 250 Protestant churches in the world. Although there are a great many distinct Protestant churches made up of some 215,000,000 members, it is possible to reduce them all to perhaps ten or twelve familes. Most Protestant churches are represented in the United States, which manifests the greatest variety of Protestant belief.

Let us summarize this introductory chapter on non-Catholic Christian churches. The Catholic Church is a world-wide institution with its central authority in Rome. There are some 525,000,000 Catholics spread over the whole globe. The Eastern Orthodox churches have their main strength in the Slav countries and Greek-speaking lands. They number about 130,000,000 members. Churches of the Protestant tradition have their strength where Germanic languages are spoken: German, English, Scandinavian and Dutch. They number some 215,000,000. The Catholics make up almost 60 percent of all Christians. All non-Catholic Christians compose a fraction more than 40 percent of the total.

2. THE EASTERN ORTHODOX CHURCHES

In the ancient Church (325–450) Catholics were grouped according to regions of the Roman Empire. These regions were called patriarchates because they were each under the jurisdiction of a patriarch who was the bishop of an important city of the Roman world. The five patriarchates were Rome, Alexandria, Antioch, Jerusalem and Constantinople. With time Constantinople became the most important city of the Church because it was the imperial capital. Constantine had moved his residence from Rome to a little town called Byzantium on the European side of the straits of Bosporus. He renamed the city for himself, calling it the City of Constantine (*-ople* is from *polis*, which means city).

The five patriarchates had an order of importance, and even though Constantinople was politically the leading city, Rome was always considered the first patriarchate and its bishop was always the first bishop.

Because of the withdrawal of the Nestorians after the Council of Ephesus (431), many of the Christians of the patriarchate of Antioch left the Catholic Church and so this patriarchate lost its greatness. This was true likewise for the patriarchate of Alexandria when most of its Christians left the Church after the Council of Chalcedon (451). Jerusalem never was a great patriarchate and had received its title by reason of its connection with the life and work of Our Lord. Consequently by 500 A.D. the important patriarchates were only two, Rome and Constantinople.

Each patriarchate had its own customs, even though all shared the same faith, same sacraments, same union, and same recognition of each other. The different patriarchates performed the sacraments in different languages and with different rites, though they were the same sacraments everywhere. The rites and customs of the patriarchate of Constantinople were called Byzantine because the city was originally called Byzantium. The rites of the Roman patriarchate were called the

7

Roman or Latin rite, for from about the third century its language was Latin.

As the eastern half of the Roman Empire continued without much change with Greek as its language, the western half became greatly changed with many tongues. The Germanic tribes slowly became absorbed into union but in the process the color and feeling of the west became different from that of the east. In consequence there were frequent frictions between the eastern and western halves of the Catholic Church. The two halves no longer understood each other. The last friction produced the break between the churches which has continued to our time. The great and tragic moment is usually marked as 1054 when the patriarch of Constantinople, Michael Caerularius, disowned the whole Church of the West. From that time on, those Christians who followed the action of Patriarch Michael have called themselves Orthodox. Their full name is the *Orthodox Catholic Church of the East.*

The patriarchate of Constantinople had sent its missionaries to the Slav peoples as early as the 800s. The greatest of these missionaries were two brothers, SS. Cyril and Methodius, who did their work in the ninth century. Though the saints were Byzantines, they worked in collaboration with the Roman Pontiff. The final outcome was that the Lithuanians and western Slavs (Poles, Moravians, Czechs, Croats and Slovaks) adhered to Roman rites and customs while the Romanians and eastern Slavs (Russians, Ukranians, Bulgars) followed the rites of Constantinople, but using their own languages in the liturgy.

After the split in 1054 the eastern Slavs remained with Constantinople. Hence the bulk of Orthodox Christians is Slavic, not Greek. Yet the first patriarch for the Orthodox is the Greek patriarch of Constantinople, but he does not have the right to command any Orthodox churches other than the relatively small church of Constantinople. For all Orthodox churches he holds the first place of honor but not the first place of command.

The Orthodox form their churches by nationalities. There

8

is the Russian Church, the Rumanian Church, the Bulgarian Church, etc. All of them together make up the Orthodox Catholic Church of the East. They are not in union with the Roman Catholic Church, nor do they recognize the Bishop of Rome (Pope) as the jurisdictional and infallible head of the Church.

In doctrine they are very much like the Roman Catholic Church. They say the same creeds, use the same sacraments, have the same general structure of belief and worship. They have bishops, priests, monks and nuns. Their Mass is fundamentally just like the Catholic Mass but they call it the Holy Liturgy. This Liturgy is celebrated not according to the Roman Rite but according to the ancient Byzantine Rite. They use bread with yeast in it for communion. (Catholic hosts are made just of flour and water without yeast.) Any language can be used, so that the Liturgy is celebrated in Greek, Old Slavonic, Arabic, Romanian, English, German, etc. The Liturgy is much longer than the Roman Mass and an Orthodox church hides its altar behind a wall on which there are pictures of Christ, Our Lady and the Saints. They give communion both in bread and wine. But the parts of the Mass are perfectly visible in the Orthodox Liturgy. There is the epistle and gospel; offertory; consecration; prayers for the living and dead; Our Father; communion; blessing.

The Orthodox have great devotion to Our Lady and the saints. They have stricter fast days than Catholics do, nor do they eat meat on Fridays. They have two kinds of clergy: married and unmarried. Like Catholics, they do not allow a priest to get married, but on the other hand they will ordain married men who continue to live as married men. The bishops are always unmarried, and so also are monks.

In doctrine the Orthodox reject the primacy of the Pope in teaching and rule. They have different views concerning the procession of the Holy Ghost — a very subtle doctrine. They do not believe in Purgatory but they pray for the dead. They teach that the Blessed Virgin is absolutely sinless but they deny the Catholic doctrine on the Immaculate Conception.

9

They recognize all the Church Councils up to 787 but do not accept those which were held after that date. Some of the Orthodox do not use our ordinary calendar called Gregorian after Pope Gregory XIII (1502–1585) who made it the calendar of the Church. The result is that the Easter feast days do not usually coincide with the Catholic dates. The Orthodox follow the older calendar called Julian because of Julius Caesar who made it the calendar for the Roman Empire.

In the United States there are more than a dozen Orthodox churches. They share the same faith and worship but they have no other strong union among themselves. Three are Russian churches not in union with each other. Likewise there are four Ukrainian churches. The most conspicuous is the Greek church. In addition there are Romanian, Syrian, Bulgarian, Albanian, Serbian churches. Altogether there are over 3,000,000 Orthodox Christians in thousands of parishes within the United States and they form one of the four major faiths of the country — Protestant, Catholic, Jewish and Orthodox.

The Orthodox in the United States live for the most part in the larger cities of the east, mid-west and Pacific coast. Catholics should have special affection for these Christians. Our church recognizes the validity of Orthodox ordinations to the episcopate and priesthood. We also recognize the validity of their sacraments. Their Liturgy is as valid as our Mass. In danger of death a Catholic could go to confession to an Orthodox priest and receive from him Extreme Unction and Communion if there were no Catholic priest available. An Orthodox Christian on becoming a Catholic is not rebaptized nor reconfirmed. He simply makes his confession of sins since his last confession in the Orthodox church.

Not all the Orthodox churches follow the same customs. Russians have variations not to be found among the Greeks. Today the tendency is growing stronger to celebrate the Liturgy in English. Churches with the "onion dome," a cupola shaped like an onion surmounted with a cross having three cross bars, are typical of Slavic Orthodox churches but are not used by the Greeks. Formerly all their priests wore beards but today in America many Orthodox priests are clean-shaven. Outside of divine services they will wear the Roman collar just like Catholic priests. They are to be addressed as "Father."

Catholics are intensely interested in reunion with the Eastern Orthodox. Their life of worship is quite the same as ours. In doctrine only a little separates us, but that little is stubborn. Catholics should look with special love on the Orthodox and they should pray that both Catholics and Orthodox become one as they were in the days of the ancient Church.

3. ROMAN CATHOLICS OF THE EASTERN RITES

To prevent mistakes, it is necessary to point out that there are Roman Catholics who in their worship and customs act exactly like non-Catholic Christians of the different oriental rites although they are thoroughly and formally Catholics. In the last chapter we looked at the Eastern Orthodox churches. With very few exceptions they all use the Byzantine rite, the ancient rite of Byzantium which is the older name for the city of Constantinople. There are Roman Catholics who use this same liturgy. Sometimes they are called Uniates because they are in union with the Catholic Church to which they belong. However, this name is not liked by them because the word has been used as a word of contempt by non-Catholic easterners. Hence it is better not to use that name but to call them, as they do themselves, *Roman Catholics of the Byzantine Rite*.

This chapter is, therefore, a postscript to the chapter on the Eastern Orthodox and deals with those Catholics who do not follow the Latin rite in their religious life. They *are* Catholics. They do not celebrate Mass and the sacraments in the way of western Catholics but use the forms made in the ancient patriarchates of the East when they were one with Rome. Any Catholic can attend their services; receive communion under both bread and wine in their Masses; go to confession at any

11

time to their priests. This is also true the other way round. They can go to Latin services and receive Communion and the sacraments from Latin rite priests. In America we find many Catholics of the Eastern Rites attending Catholic schools and joining Catholic societies which in their worship use only the Latin rite. Latin rite Catholics should show the highest respect for Catholics of the Eastern Rites. The history of these easterners is glorious and they have suffered very much because of their simultaneous adherence both to the Catholic Church and their ancestral eastern liturgies. In all of these churches there are married clergy, though in the United States most of their priests are unmarried. It will be the privilege of not a few Latin Catholics to know sons and daughters of priests of Oriental Catholic parishes. Latin rite Catholics should take the opportunity to attend Mass in such churches and have their friends explain it to them. The Eastern Rite Masses are all very beautiful. The vestments are somewhat different from what Latins know in their own churches. The music is quite distinct from the Gregorian chant of the Latin worship. The language will not be Latin. It cannot be emphasized too much that these Catholics are in no way less Catholic than those of the Latin rite. For the good of both groups the greatest amount of union and friendship is necessary. Latin rite Catholic high schools should from time to time invite an Eastern Rite Catholic priest to celebrate the eastern liturgies so that the whole school can see the Mass done in a different dress.

There are about 15,000,000 Roman Catholics in the world who use one or other of the Eastern Rites in their religious life and worship. In America there are over 900,000. They have their own priests, nuns and bishops. Every large city has churches which are the centers of their Catholic life. These should be visited by all Catholics in order that they may know each other better.

Perhaps there are individual Catholics of all Eastern Rites in our land. However, some of the rites do not have their own churches in this country. There are no Copt churches, no Ethiopian churches, no churches for Malabar Catholics.

Catholics of such rites will use the ordinary Latin churches in the region where they live. But the Ukrainians, Ruthenians, Armenians, Chaldeans, Melkites, Romanians, and Maronites in many places have their proper churches and chapels. Cities like New York, Chicago, Detroit and San Francisco have many such congregations.

The most numerous Eastern Rite Catholics in the United States are the *Ukrainians* and *Ruthenians*. There are two Ukrainian dioceses, Philadelphia and Stamford, Conn., with their own bishops for the Ukrainian Catholics of the country. The Ruthenians have one diocese to which all belong and their bishop lives in Pittsburgh. There are about 325,000 Ukrainian Catholics in the United States and about 225,000 Ruthenians.

In our time all these Catholics are American born and bred. But their ancestors came from Middle Europe. The Ukrainians are not from the Russian Ukraine but from the Polish province of Galizia. The Ruthenians — a word which comes from Latin and means Russian — come from the Carpathian mountain area of Czecho-Slovakia. Neither group is Russian in the sense that they belonged to the lands ordinarily called Russian. In blood they are, however, related to the South Russian peoples. They do not speak Russian but Polish, Czech or Russin. There never has been, nor is there now, a Russian Catholic Church, though there are a few Catholic churches in modern Russia, and these are mainly of the Latin rite.

In the homelands of the Ukrainian and Ruthenian Catholics, the Soviet government has forced them all to be under the Russian Orthodox Church. We can easily suppose that this has not changed the faith of most of the people, but they cannot worship in independence.

In the United States they have a vigorous church-life. They follow the Byzantine rite and some of their clergy are married. In the Liturgy (Mass) they use Church Slavonic as it is called, an old form of the language of the Slavs, and therefore somewhat different from any of the Slav languages in current use. The trend today is to use much English. Though many of these churches still have the iconostasis (the picture wall between the altar and the people) some have removed it so that the church looks more like a Latin rite church. But by rule there should be no statues, stations of the cross, confessionals or holy water fonts. There ought not be Benediction of the Blessed Sacrament. Some churches have nevertheless introduced it. There should be no organ, and the choirs sing beautifully with no accompaniment. Communion is in both wine and yeasted bread. Confirmation is given by the priest at the time of baptism. Confessions are heard at the iconastasis with the priest standing at the central door. (There are, however, local variations.) They have their own parochial schools, high schools and colleges.

In addition to the Ukrainians and Ruthenians there are Byzantine rite Catholics called *Melkites*. These descend from Syrians, of Syria, Mesopotamia and Palestine in Asia. Their forefathers were once Greek Orthodox but in the course of the centuries they became united to Rome. Their head is the Melkite Patriarch of Antioch, who lives in Damascus. There are less than 400,000 of them in the world, of whom more than fifty thousand live in the United States. Except for minor variations, they have the same Byzantine rite used by the Ukrainians and Ruthenians, but their liturgical language is usually Arabic. However, the American Melkites also manifest the tendency to use more and more English in the liturgy.

Eastern Rite Catholics using liturgies different from the Byzantine are of course many, but only three groups are evident in the United States. These are the *Maronites, Armenians* and *Chaldeans*. The Maronites have their home center in the Lebanon, Syria, and they have been in union with Rome almost from the beginning. Their church worship looks quite like Latin services, though the structure of their Mass is really different. In this country none of their clergy is married and they give communion in bread alone. Their liturgical language is mainly Arabic. There are about 900,000 of them in the whole world under the Maronite Patriarch of Antioch, residing in Beirut, Lebanon.

In this country there may be as many as 300,000 Maronites and they have almost fifty parishes. Though their true head is their own patriarch in Syria, they are subject to the local Latin rite bishops.

All Armenians are Christians but the greater part of the nation belongs to the *Armenian Gregorian Church* which is not in union with Rome. But one-third of the people belong to the Roman Catholic Church and they have the same Armenian liturgy which the Gregorian Armenians use. There are altogether about 200,000 Catholic Armenians of whom some 25,000 live in the United States. In this country they have six parishes whose head is the Catholic Armenian Patriarch, who is called "Katholikos." He resides in Beirut, Lebanon. American Catholic Armenians, however, are under the authority of the local Latin rite bishops.

Armenian liturgy, celebrated in classical Armenian, is substantially Byzantine but it has undergone many Latin variations. At certain parts of the Mass a curtain should be drawn before the whole sanctuary but in this country this practice is dropped. Communion is given in bread alone.

There are not many Chaldean Catholics in the country. They have two parishes, one in Chicago and one in Detroit. They follow the Antiochian rite according to the East Syrian usage. The language of the liturgy is Arabic and Eastern Syriac. The Mass does not appear too unlike the Latin Mass and the altar is like a Latin altar. In all there are some 175,000 Chaldean Catholics in the world, of whom less than 3000 live in America. Their homeland is in Iraq, Iran and Syria.

4. THE PROTESTANT CHURCHES

We have seen that the Catholic Church was one always. In 1054 the eastern half went its own way, claiming however to be the Catholic Church though it called itself the Orthodox Church. The separation took place on geographic lines so that there were no Orthodox in the west. But the Catholic Church in the sixteenth century was faced with secession within its own geographical territory.

From the thirteenth century onwards there were little groups in the west which splintered off from Catholic solidarity. They were called Albigensians, Waldensians, Spirituals, Lollards and Hussites. Western Europe was one commonwealth, and unity of faith was the constitutional basis of the union. In consequence the total community treated the new men as traitors to the general unity and they were persecuted. But the little movements, which were alive only in narrow separated localities, did take place all over the western European commonwealth: France, Italy, England and Bohemia. These little cracks prepared the grounds for a wide-spread separation in the sixteenth century.

The man who triggered off the great division was Martin Luther. He was a German and a priest of the Church. He belonged to the mendicant order of the Augustinian Friars. (He was not technically a monk.) He was a most interesting man with great force of character and personality. In all of his life religion was his main concern. In his studies and personal anxieties he reached two conclusions. The first was that the Bible alone was enough as a source of doctrine, and the second that faith alone made man right with God. Now he did not understand by the word faith merely an intellectual assent to the revelation of God but rather a whole-souled trust in God's decision to save all who lovingly trusted in him. Luther was highly aware of Original Sin, that force working in man whereby we are led to sin. Original Sin was in all men and it worked on every thing man did. Hence man was always sinning. He could not do the good he wished but rather did the evil he did not want. This could not be changed, but God was willing to save man anyhow because of God's goodness. This goodness was made clear in the life and death of the God-man Jesus Christ. What God wants from man is trust because of Jesus Christ.

It was pointed out to Luther that he was not giving the

full doctrine of the Church in this grave matter. He left out some things which were important. Luther however felt that his doctrine was the basic teaching of the Bible and he thought that the Bible alone was enough. Only that church-doctrine was necessary which the individual Christian could find for himself in the Bible. The individual Christian was under the influence of the Holy Ghost and with the Spirit's enlightening he could learn the mind of God from the Scriptures. By this method what was found in the Bible was Catholic truth and anything else was either false or useless.

Luther had no intention of leaving the Catholic Church. When officials of the Church condemned his doctrines and expelled him, he was surprised and angered. He came to the conclusion that the Roman Catholic Church was a corruption of the Church of Christ which was still invisibly here in spite of visible corruptions. He wished therefore to cling to Christ's Church and rid it of Roman deformations. It is important to remember that Luther never wanted to found a new church. He thoroughly believed that the Church of Christ was here and did not need to be founded. He only wished to reorganize its congregations so that the purity of the primitive Church was maintained. Such congregations were to be reformed congregations of the Church of Christ — they were not in Luther's intention a Lutheran church. In his mind he was not making something new but rather cleaning up the old.

As a matter of fact Luther did found a new church. The old church rejected Lutheran changes and those congregations which accepted the Lutheran teaching soon became a church of their own. With time one could speak of a Lutheran church and today we do speak in this way.

Luther's teaching stimulated other men to think along his lines. In nearby north Switzerland a Swiss priest by the name of Hulderich (Ulrich) Zwingli started reforms but his ideas were far more radical than Luther's, and Luther did not like him. Zwingli died early in the battle but his work was taken over by a French layman, John Calvin, whose headquarters were in Geneva in south Switzerland. Calvin believed that true

17

believers could act virtuously by God's blessing and that they should form civic communities which were the embodiment of God's will for man. But the Lutherans did not approve of Calvinism as the doctrines of Calvin were called. The two branches of the reform took on different names and a mutual hostility developed. Lutherans were called Evangelicals and Calvinists were called the Reformed. Lutheranism spread from north Germany into Denmark, Sweden, Norway and Finland. Calvinism settled in Switzerland and moved into France, Holland and Scotland.

In England Henry VIII, an enemy of Luther, kept the Catholic faith but separated the English church from obedience to the Pope of Rome, making himself the head of the Church in England. It is not true to say that Henry founded any church or that he reformed the Anglican Church. He merely cut it off from the jurisdiction of the Roman See. During the reign of his only son, the boy Edward VI, and mainly in the reign of his daughter, Elizabeth I, the Church of England was reformed by statesmen and theologians. However the English reform was far more moderate than the reform on the European continent, and Luther's doctrines were not made basic. Both Zwingli and Calvin were influential but there was a strong tendency to retain much of the ancient Catholic tradition both in doctrine and worship. Above all the system of bishops as rulers of the church was retained, which was not true in Lutheranism and Calvinism.

The fourth expression of reform never became geographically organized and its champions were persecuted by the other three reforming groups. This fourth group is sometimes called Anabaptist, and also Ecstatics or Free Spirits. They were called Anabaptist because in Greek this word means to baptize again. They did not accept the baptism of infants and baptized converts who had already been baptized. They were disturbingly prominent in Germany and both Luther and Calvin detested them. They believed in the direct action of the Spirit on believers and they were guided by the Inner Light with little con-

18

cern for rulers and church leaders. They did not consolidate anywhere but their ideas never died out in Protestantism. In spite of their name, they are not historically connected with our modern Baptists.

Such were the four movements of the Protestant reform. The name Protestant comes from the civil protest which princes who had joined the reforming movement raised at the imperial Diet of Speyer in 1529. They protested against the laws restricting their efforts at spreading their doctrines. The name soon after became general and accepted by the reformers themselves. (There was at this time another reform movement which was Catholic and brought forth the great reform Council of Trent, 1545–63. We must therefore always distinguish between Catholic Reformation and Protestant Reformation.)

As can be seen from what has been said, Protestantism is not a church. It is a principle understood differently by different Protestant church unions. Protestantism is one only in general principle, not in organization nor even in beliefs and worship. There can be endless varieties of Protestant churches nor should we look for much unity among them. Yet from the original four movements all Protestant churches derive. However, they need not descend by a straight continuous line from one original movement. The four movements crisscross producing new churches in the course of time. Older churches die and new ones are born. It is quite impossible to say exactly how many there are, but it can be safely said that there are approximately 250 of them.

To help us to be clear, we speak of denominations, churches and sects. A denomination is the name given to different (and even hostile) churches because all share somehow in a definite particular vision of Christian faith and life of some past churchman or historical church group. Thus there are many churches which are called by one name. The Baptists are a denomination. The Lutherans are a denomination. The Presbyterians are a denomination. A church is an organized union of different congregations within one denomination.

Thus the Southern Baptist Convention is one Baptist church alongside others of the same denomination. If the union is large or fairly large, we call it a church; if it is quite small and not conspicuous, we call it a sect.

In the following twenty-three chapters we will deal with Protestant denominations and the more prominent Protestant Churches of America.

5. THE LUTHERAN CHURCHES

Since Martin Luther was the first to propose and execute a Protestant reform of the Church, we may well begin the descriptions of Protestant churches by speaking of the Lutherans. There are two Lutheran principles which have to be accepted in order to be a Lutheran believer. These are that man is made right with God by faith alone, and that the Bible alone expresses the divine teaching for men. These principles are fundamental for any Lutheran church but they can of course be understood in different ways. In order to keep down the variety of understandings Lutherans drew up official explanations. In the lifetime of Luther and shortly afterwards certain documents were written as the true expressions of Lutheran faith.

Among the official explanations are to be found two catechisms which Luther himself wrote: the Longer and Shorter. The most important explanation of Lutheranism is the Augsburg Confession which was presented to Emperor Charles V at the imperial Diet of Augsburg in 1530. This document was written by Philipp Melanchthon, Luther's scholarly collaborator, and it was seen and approved by Luther himself. All Lutherans hold this Confession in high regard. In it is stated that Lutherans accept the famous creeds of Christendom: the Apostles' Creed, the Nicene Creed (which Catholics say or sing at all Sunday masses), and the Athanasian Creed. After the death of Luther in 1546 there was confusion in

Lutheran circles, with great differences of opinion on what must be believed. To solve this problem Lutheran theologians published in 1580 the Concordia or Formula of Concord which met with universal acceptation.

Thus we see that the great explanations of Lutheran belief are the three creeds of the ancient Church, the Augsburg Confession and the Formula of Concord. (There are others, too, but these five are the main official explanations.)

The Lutherans have a difficulty arising from these official explanations. These writings are normative for Lutheran faith and yet the first principle of Lutheran doctrine is that the Bible alone is the authoritative teaching of the Church. Lutherans solve the difficulty by stating that these creeds truly state the biblical message.

In general it can be said that Lutherans believe in the Trinity, one God in three distinct divine persons; the divinity and humanity of Jesus Christ; the atoning death of Christ for all men; the presence of an evil force in all men called Original Sin; salvation through trust in Christ's merits alone; the lack of any merit in man; the invisible union of all true believers which is the Church; the sufficiency of the Bible alone for Church-teaching; the use of two sacraments — baptism and the Lord's Supper.

In their worship there are two kinds of service. One is the service of the Word in which prayer, hymn singing and the sermon on the Gospel are the components. The other is the Supper or Communion service. In the latter the sermon is not omitted but the service is a modification of the Roman Mass with Communion given in both kinds. Until recently American Lutherans did not celebrate the Lord's Supper very often but in our time there is a strong movement toward liturgical worship which is more and more like the Catholic Mass. (In Sweden a Lutheran High Mass with Roman vestments has always been traditional in many churches for Sunday worship.) In consequence the Supper is now frequently celebrated. In the Supper Service the Kyrie, Gloria, Nicene Creed, Sanctus, Benedictus and Agnus Dei are sung in English. In the matter

21

of vestments there is variation, but the use of cassock, surplice and stole is common. Some ministers use alb and chasuble.

Since the days of Luther congregational singing is a great feature of Lutheran worship. It is wonderful to hear a whole congregation singing old liturgical hymns or more modern songs with might and main.

Lutherans believe in the universal priesthood of all believers. Hence for them ordination is not a sacrament but only the appointment of a believer to direct worship and church life. Ordination however is given by other ministers imposing hands on the candidate. The ordained man does not cease to be a layman and his ordination does not give him special powers but only a definite task.

Unlike most Protestants, Lutherans believe in the real physical presence of Christ in the Eucharist, but they reject the Catholic doctrine of Transubstantiation. Nor do they in general keep the Sacrament in the church outside of services.

In Germany and the Scandinavian countries Lutheranism was the state religion. This is no longer true in the German Republic. In the old days, therefore, the Lutheran churches were organized by the government. For a definite district some minister was appointed to be chief overseer. In Norway and Sweden he always was called the bishop. Until Hitler's time, the word bishop was not used in Germany, but today it is. In America the Lutherans are reluctant to give the presidents of their synods or churches the title of bishop, though they may well do so in the near future. However, even when the title is used, there is no intention of stating that the holder of the title is any more than a higher functionary of the church. It does not imply apostolic succession or special supernatural power. Luther, who rejected the notion of the episcopate as a divinely instituted office, had no objection to the use of the *word* bishop but he did not introduce it himself.

Confession to a pastor is optional, not necessary, for the Lutheran confesses to God who in his goodness does not hold the sin against the believer. There are Lutherans today, especially in Germany, called High Church Lutherans and these

22

urge people to confess to the pastor. When confession is made, there is a liturgical absolution of sins. But the general Lutheran opinion is that Confession is not a sacrament nor is it necessary. It is a good thing if one wants it.

Confirmation is given to young people as a sign of their entry into the full responsibility of church life. It is not considered a sacrament and it will be given by the pastor of the congregation. Marriage is celebrated in the churches but is not a sacrament. Ministers, of course, are usually married. Extreme Unction, except among some High Church Lutherans, is not used.

Lutherans believe in the saints mentioned in the Bible. They do not canonize new ones. They name their churches after saints: Peter, Paul, Luke, John, Stephen, etc. Mary, the mother of Christ, is a saint, but Lutherans do not like to call her the Mother of God. They do not believe in her Immaculate Conception or Assumption. There is no prayer to the saints, only to God and his Christ, yet in their churches they have pictures and even statues. All modern Lutheran churches likewise have a sanctuary. In its center is a simple altar with candles and a cross on it.

In outlining Lutheran faith and worship, there was no intention to say that all Lutherans accept all these things. For over a century it has been common in Lutheran churches for many, especially among the learned, to be very free in belief. There have been and there are Lutherans whose faith is not at all orthodox. Many do not believe that Christ was truly the Son of God as the Nicene Creed teaches. Some do not believe in a physical afterlife. The notion of miracles and the supernatural is sometimes rejected. There is no supposition that the Bible is without error or that it is really the word of God. In some Lutheran churches such men and women would be expelled, but in many more they are not disturbed.

Even though the last paragraph is quite true, it must nonetheless be said that the Lutherans in general are anxious to keep the ancient faith. Lutherans really care about right doctrine, which is not true in some Protestant churches.

23

In matters of morality they have an excellent record. Although they permit divorce, they discourage it. They preach and practise sobriety, simplicity, honesty, chastity, neighborliness and piety. Lutheran churches often have their own parochial schools, high schools and colleges to insure the religious education of their youth. Among non-Catholic churches which maintain parochial schools in the U.S., only Lutherans have a nation-wide system comparable to the Catholic one.

Lutherans also have their own hospitals and homes conducted by Lutheran deaconesses. The deaconesses are Lutheran women somewhat like Catholic nursing sisters, but they take no vows and may get married. When they do, they leave the diaconate. While deaconesses they are either unmarried or widows.

6. LUTHERAN CHURCHES IN AMERICA

The country called the United States of America had as an important part of its beginnings the groups of immigrants who came from England in the seventeenth century. They were English and brought with them the English religions of their time. England was never Lutheran nor were there ever many Lutherans in the land. Hence they did not import Lutheranism into this country. But Lutherans from the German lands and Sweden did come to America, and at a relatively early date. These settled in Pennsylvania and Delaware. All through the nineteenth century a steady stream of Lutherans from different European countries came to the New World. The result is that today the Lutherans number over eight million in America. They make up the third largest Protestant denomination in the United States, coming after the Baptists and Methodists.

The denomination is large but it is not organically united. At one time there were as many as 150 Lutheran churches in this country, but during this century the movement is toward fusing the churches into larger and fewer unions. It is not improbable that by the year 2000 there will be only two Lutheran churches in the whole country, although there are at least eighteen at present. The reason why there are so many Lutheran churches here is because of the many lands from which the first Lutherans came. When they arrived in their new homes they united together by language. Hence German, Danish, Norwegian, Swedish, Finnish, and Slovak churches came into being. The Germans were the largest segment of American Lutheranism though they did not form one church but many regional churches.

There are two over-all federations to which most but not all Lutheran churches belong. One is the Lutheran World Federation with its headquarters in Geneva, Switzerland. This association of Lutheran churches works closely with the World Council of Churches. Within our own country there is the National Lutheran Council. Again not all Lutheran churches of America have joined. These two federations are not churches but uniting agencies of separated churches. But their influence will be to bring the distinct churches into organic union.

Of the eighteen or more Lutheran churches in America three stand out by reason of numbers and distinctive spirit. They are the *United Lutheran Church in America*, the *Lutheran Church–Missouri Synod*, and the *American Lutheran Church*. In the light of the strong trend toward mergers within Lutheranism, it is safe to say that these three churches will in ten years include nine-tenths of all American Lutherans.

American Lutheranism is distinguished from that of the original Lutheran churches of the motherlands in that it has a strongly congregational consciousness. In Germany under the emperors church doctrine and policy were centrally determined. The local congregation followed the decisions of the governmental church ministry since the Lutheran churches were national churches. A high degree of unity was thus achieved. In America Lutherans entered into a community which had no governmental concern for religion. In consequence the Lutherans formed their local congregations with or without help from the motherland. The notion of a ruling office within the Church given sacramentally is alien to Lutheran doctrine. Lutherans believe in the universal priesthood of all Christian believers. Now when everyone is priest, no one is a hierarch. The church is made up only of laymen. If a government takes over the administration of the churches, the congregations are united by governmental authority but this is not so if each congregation leads its own life. When the Lutherans came to this country they had to form local congregations rather than insert themselves into a church already existing. It was only after the existence of many independent congregations that the parishes could unite. The union, of course, was a matter of congregational decision and different kinds of union were possible. The union makes a church, not the mere existence of isolated congregations.

The attractiveness of union is felt by all men. There was therefore an antecedent pull in the Lutheran congregations to unite into churches. Unions could be formed on different bases. Common language and common origins were natural bonds of union. A common locality is also a natural unifying force. Common understanding of official declarations of doctrine will make groups one. Language and origin did bring Lutheran congregations together but today, more and more, there is only one language in the whole land and only one American consciousness. Hence this force toward union will not produce separate churches. Likewise localities are no longer divisive. The country is becoming more and more one place with easy transportation and movement from region to region. Hence regionalism is weaker now than formerly. But different views of doctrine are still with us. Doctrine will divide the churches, and in Lutheranism it does.

The two largest Lutheran churches in the country are the United Lutheran Church and the Lutheran Church–Missouri Synod. They are separated by doctrine but their separation is typically American. In Europe, especially in Germany, great leeway is given to Lutherans in the matter of belief. This began in the nineteenth century when so many Lutheran thinkers denied many of the positions of Martin Luther including fundamental doctrines like the divinity of Christ, the truth of his resurrection, his birth of Mary ever Virgin, etc. Against this school of thinkers another group was formed. They were called in general Pietists: men and women of simple faith, dedicated to a pious Christian life. They abhorred the doctrines of the Liberals as the others were called. By and large the German Lutherans who came to America were of a Pietist mentality. They staunchly accepted Lutheran doctrine according to the Lutheran confessional explanations. They were quite literal in their understanding of the Bible. They were conservative of the old ways which they had inherited from their fathers.

The nineteenth century produced great variety of theology in Protestantism and Lutheranism. As a result many American Lutheran thinkers dropped the simpler attitudes of the Pietists. These men and women were not too conservative and they gave much room for different interpretations of the Bible and the confessional explanations.

In consequence Lutheranism in America was divided into three segments: the Conservatives, the Liberals, and those somewhere in between. It was natural that church unions should be made in the light of these differences.

American Lutherans in general find no attraction in a revolutionary Liberalism. They do not want to throw over the historical doctrines of the early Lutheran reform. Hence the question is only how far one must keep what was handed down. Those who are quite strict and want little or no change will be inclined to join the Lutheran Church–Missouri Synod. This church is very conservative and keeps watch over its pastors lest they move far away from a literal understanding of the Bible and of the confessional statements. Although other Lutheran churches are today greatly interested in liturgical worship and frequent celebration of the Lord's Supper, Missouri Synod Lutherans are cautious in accepting this change. In principle they are not against it because these things were very prominent in early Lutheran times, but they were not part of the American Lutheran tradition.

The Lutheran Church–Missouri Synod is a very zealous church. There is a stubbornness in it which makes it lively. It is this church which is most interested in parochial schools, which it conducts with solidity and success.

The United Lutheran Church and the American Lutheran Church are not strictly speaking Liberal, but they do not make the same demands which the Missouri Synod does. They give their pastors, scholars and lay folk much greater freedom in matters of belief and worship. In these churches we find thinkers and preachers with ideas far more open than is the rule in the Missouri Synod. Both the United Lutheran Church and the American Lutheran Church are deeply interested in the Ecumenical Movement (the movement to bring all Christian churches into unity) and in consequence members of these churches show greater friendliness to Catholics. In the Missouri Synod there is anti-Catholicism, though it does not manifest itself in insulting, aggressive forms. In spite of this fact, this church is somewhat embarrassed because some of its most cherished beliefs are held by the Catholics, though rejected by many Lutherans.

7. THE CALVINIST CHURCHES

Since the second strain in the original Protestant reformation followed the guidance of John Calvin (1509–1564) we shall now take a look at the Protestant churches which derive from him or are heavily influenced by his teaching and example. Calvin accepted Luther's two main doctrines: 1) Man is made right with God through trusting faith alone; 2) God's mind is expressed in the Scripture alone where it is to be gathered by the individual believer enlightened by the Holy Ghost.

Calvin differed from Luther in a number of ways. The French reformer was a highly logical and orderly thinker. In his early Protestant days he wrote a clear, consistent account of his Protestant doctrine. It is called the *Institutes of the Christian Religion* (1536). Things which were mysterious in the message of God were left mysterious by Luther, who did not try to push them to a logical conclusion. But Calvin wished to get to the bottom. He was struck by the authority, majesty and power of God and creation's total dependence on him. Calvin then worked out his theory of *predestination*. God, before he created anything, decided to create some men whom he would save. He also decided to make others whom he would damn. Christ was to die for those who were predestined for salvation, not for the others. Christ's grace came to the predestined, nor could they refuse it; and having received it, they were certain of entering heaven finally. Without grace man could do no good, but with grace he could and irresistibly would.

Like Luther, Calvin admitted only two sacraments: Baptism and the Lord's Supper. Calvin did not believe that Christ is physically present in the Eucharist, but that the believer really did become one with Christ on consuming the bread and wine because of the believer's faith. (This doctrine annoyed Luther very much.)

Again like Luther, Calvin did not believe in Holy Orders. All Christians were priests, and no one was more a priest than another. However, Calvin was deeply interested in the form which the visible church should take. Luther was quite willing to have church organization framed and administered by any Christian prince in whose territory the congregations existed. For Luther the life of the Church was given by the Holy Spirit living in her, and external arrangements could easily be taken care of by the leaders of the congregation itself or by the temporal rulers if they were God-fearing Christians. Luther was mainly concerned with substantially right doctrine and substantially proper worship. He was not too preoccupied with details.

Calvin was a different kind of man. Details meant much to him. He would not leave it to each congregation to arrange its external life; much less would he leave it to the governmental rulers. He set up four orders within his church: elders of two kinds (preaching ministers of worship, and lay elders who with the ministers had ruling power over the congregation), lay teachers, and deacons. Only the elders, ministerial and lay, ruled the church, nor was the congregation independent. Each congregation sent ministerial and lay elders to a central council which directed and controlled all the congregations. The Greek word for elder is presbyter, and Calvin's church-organization is therefore called presbyterian.

Calvin's ideas of predestination and irresistible grace colored his idea of the Church of Christ. For him the Church was only for the predestined. It was of course really invisible, but through the congregation predestination and divine grace at work could be seen by the world. Not all in the visible congregation were necessarily among the elect but yet the congregation was the external manifestation of the elect. Stern virtue and divine blessing were therefore the clear mark of the Calvinistic community. It was under God and therefore could be under no human civil government, but rather human civil government was under it. The Calvinist community could not tolerate sinners, heretics or the godless. It could not tolerate any independent government for the civic business of the community. The church through its high council, which Calvin called a *consistorium*, was the final voice in all things.

The theology of Calvin ruled Geneva from 1541 until his death in 1564. From this city Calvinism was carried into France where it formed the Huguenots whose modern name is the *Reformed Evangelical Church of France*. It moved likewise into the northern Netherlands which we call Holland, and there became the state church. John Knox, a Scottish priest who dropped Catholicism, imported Calvinism into Scotland. It also penetrated into Germany, Hungary and Poland.

Calvinism had its troubles. It opposed Catholicism and was opposed by the Lutherans. This produced wars and persecutions. The Calvinist doctrine of predestination is very difficult, and for a large community the rigid demands for sobriety and stern virtue are hard to meet. A certain sternness was typical of Calvin's religion.

Calvin was not long dead when Calvinist theologians began to modify the teaching of the master. The leader of this movement was a Dutchman, Jacob Hermanas (1560–1609), who in the fashion of the time latinized his name to Arminius. The three shocking points in Calvin's doctrine are that God for his own divine pleasure decides in advance that some men will be led to heaven and others will be steered to hell. Man can do nothing about this decision and its execution. Those who are going to heaven cannot but be virtuous and those who are going to hell cannot but be vicious. The predestined are sure of their rightness with God and they cannot lose it. Arminius changed these views. He taught that God does indeed want some men to go to heaven but they freely co-operate with God's plan. It is in man's power to reject God's grace. What is more, man can receive God's grace and also lose it. There is no guarantee that he will keep it always.

From that point on Calvinists have been divided. In our days there are very few who accept Calvin's doctrines on predestination, although some of their churches may have the doctrine in their basic books of teaching. What distinguishes modern Calvinist churches is their principle of organization, or polity as it is called. It is neither aristocratic nor democratic. Presbyterians reject decisively the notion of a bishop's office in the Church. Of course the *name* does not annoy them. What they cannot accept is the idea that God gives special empowering to some men in the church whereby they rule by divine authority. For the Calvinist of any shade of allegiance to his doctrine, God alone has authority. Problems of the congregations will be solved by the congregations themselves, who act by selecting learned and prudent men for deciding issues. This is a middle way between aristocracy and democracy. No one man has authority — it must belong to the whole congregation — but the congregation does not act immediately: it chooses good and wise men to act in its name.

Ordination within Calvinism is the congregation choosing a worthy member to be the agent of the whole body for purposes of teaching, worship and general discipline. It is done by the imposing of hands by ministers. Calvinist churches are staunchly lay churches and in their deliberative meetings laymen are as conspicuous as ordained ministers. Although in the past they did not ordain women for the ministry, today many Calvinist churches do. In Calvinism the minister did not assume any dress which would distinguish him from the rest of the congregation. Even in service of worship he wore no distinctive garb, though little by little he did use the academic cap and gown which were signs of scholarship rather than superiority in the church. Today, however, not a few Presbyterian ministers will wear the Roman collar, and the cassock is proper dress for church worship. The liturgical movement has entered into Presbyterian churches, which means that ministers will gradually take on some priestly features.

In general Calvinistic worship is very sober. Today Calvinist churches follow the styles of church architecture in general use in our country and the new churches have an altar fixed in what Catholics would call the sanctuary and Protestants call the presbytery or chancel. This was not true formerly, when no altar was visible and a table was brought in when Communion service was held — and that was a rare event, barely four times a year. (This usage can still be found.) The pulpit was the central adornment of the church hall. And it was a hall. There were no pictures, no statues, no crosses. Calvinistic worship was centered on the invisible God alone, with his Word resting on the pulpit lectern.

Although interest in liturgy is growing among Calvinists, the typical service is still severe. All Protestant services are ultimately derived from Catholic services. In Catholicism there are two liturgical actions: the sung Office which monks and canons sing, and secondly the Mass and sacraments. Protestants took their service from the sung Office rather than from the Mass. The present service will in general be true to the following outline. In the beginning there is a general call to prayer given by the minister in a prayer of invocation of God, the singing of a psalm or hymn by congregation or choir, reading or readings from the Bible, the Our Father sung or said, offerings of the people, the sermon, and a blessing prayer by the minister for all. This thin skeleton permits variation and additions but the skeleton stays. In general, Protestants sit and stand in worship. They do not kneel. Calvinists as a rule will not use the sign of the cross ever. Prayers said in public are made up by the one who prays and are not a formula set in some book of ritual.

8. THE PRESBYTERIAN CHURCHES

Calvinism produced five great denominations. They were the Reformed churches of Switzerland, Germany and Hungary; the Reformed Evangelical Churches of France; the Dutch Reformed Church; the Presbyterian churches of Scotland, England, Ireland; and the Congregationalist Churches. From England, Scotland and Ireland Presbyterianism came to the English-speaking new world. Most of the colonies of British America were officially Anglican, but they were Anglicans of heavy Calvinist persuasion. In New England the Pilgrim Fathers were Congregationalists, a genuinely Calvinist church. Even the Anglicans of New England were Puritans, which means that they were the extreme Calvinistic wing of the Church of England. Concerning the Congregationalists we shall speak in another chapter.

The Scots and the Scotch-Irish brought the Presbyterian church to America. In Scotland the Calvinistic churches called themselves Presbyterian because these churches were governed by presbyters or elders. The tradition of these Protestants was intensely anti-Catholic but they had no love for the Anglicans either, whom they considered to be Catholics in disguise. In America the Presbyterians did not move into consolidated Anglican territory. Even though New England was heavily Calvinist, the Presbyterians entered New York and Pennsylvania, and gradually followed the Blue Ridge Mountains into the South. From these mountains they penetrated into the West. Just as the Congregationalists founded Harvard and Yale for the training of their ministers, the Presbyterians started Princeton, first called the College of New Jersey.

During the American Revolution the Presbyterians, imbued with little love for the British Crown, fervently supported the cause of independence. The consequence was that the new republic esteemed them highly. Their members did well in America, and, after the Congregationalists, they are today the second wealthiest denomination in the country.

In our day the Presbyterians have not yet succeeded in uniting into one church. In fact there are ten different Presbyterian churches, but only two of them are large: the *Presbyterian Church in the United States*, and the *United Presbyterian Church in the United States of America*. The United Church has more than 3,000,000 members and the other has about a million. The larger church is the result of a merger in 1958 in which the United Presbyterian Church in the United States of America and the United Presbyterian Church of North America became one. The smaller church is the Presbyterian church of the South which separated from the northern church at the time of the Civil War.

Of the minor Presbyterian churches, perhaps the most interesting is the little *Orthodox Presbyterian Church*. It has less than 10,000 members, but it is significant. In the twenties and thirties of this century American Protestantism was faced with a serious crisis. It was a controversy between Fundamentalists and Modernists. Those were the names used but they were not apt. The question was whether the Bible was to be understood according to the obviously natural intent of the words or whether newer meanings could be constructed on the Biblical message, even if it went counter to the obvious meaning of the words themselves. The trend among Protestant theologians was toward a freer interpretation of Biblical affirmations than the Protestant past had permitted. Fundamentalists demanded that the five fundamentals of Protestantism be accepted by all. These were: the error-free nature of the in-

34

spired Bible; the birth of Jesus of a Virgin; the true divinity of Jesus; the atoning value of his death; the historical reality of his resurrection and the future coming of Christ to judge the living and the dead. Many Protestant theologians would not admit these propositions in a literal sense and against such thinkers the Fundamentalists raised their protest. One of the most intelligent of the Fundamentalists was the Presbyterian, J. Gresham Machen, formerly of Princeton Theological Seminary, which is the best known of all Presbyterian schools of divinity. Machen left Princeton and opened his own seminary in Philadelphia, and in 1936 he and his associates started the Orthodox Presbyterian Church.

The importance of Machen's work was not in the church he founded. Rather it was in the smallness of this church. Presbyterians by and large did not follow this conservative thinker. American Presbyterianism is not anxious about orthodoxy: it is neither passionately for it nor against it. The larger churches present the Westminster Confession as the creedal statement of their belief. This was a document prepared in London in 1647 by an assembly of theologians summoned by the Puritan parliament. Actually it was a genuinely Calvinistic statement, retaining strict Calvinist positions on predestination and the organization of the Church.

Even though this confession is accepted by the larger Presbyterian churches in America, few Presbyterians will follow it or believe in it altogether. They accept it as an historical statement of the past rather than as an adequate statement of present Presbyterian beliefs. It would be quite impossible to state just what is the faith of the Presbyterian churches in our time. They believe in an evangelical worship like that outlined in the preceding chapter. They cling to the representative form of church-government. They represent a gentle conservatism in morals, but they are not opposed to change.

Since the most typical thing about the Presbyterians is their church-government, we might describe its outline. The local congregation is the basis of any Presbyterian church. But the congregation is not self-standing. It belongs to a larger

35

union. The local congregation is a *session* and is governed by elders — minister and ruling elders. (The minister is a teaching elder and the laymen are ruling elders elected by the congregation. Both kinds of elders are ordained.)

The session is by no means independent. It is under the jurisdiction of the *presbytery* which is a union of 20 or 30 sessions ruled by a council made up of all the ministers of the district and lay elders, one from each session. This presbytery corresponds to a Catholic diocese and has powers much like those of a bishop. The presbyteries are in their turn united into a *synod*, which is like a Catholic Archiepiscopal Province, but its functions are not too clear. It is made up of representatives of the presbyteries. Over all the churches and councils stands the *General Assembly*, which is made up of representatives of all the presbyteries. It meets annually and decides matters of discipline, doctrine and worship. It is the ultimate tribunal for the whole church. It elects the moderator of the Assembly (equivalent to a president), and also the stated clerk (who is the executive secretary of the Assembly even after its close).

Presbyterians believe in two sacraments, Baptism and the Lord's Supper. They baptize children, who are attached to the church by the faith of their parents. This is done by pouring or sprinkling with water while the words "I baptize thee in the name of the Father, and of the Son, and of the Holy Ghost," are said.

The Supper is not celebrated too often, though the influence of the liturgical movement now gives it greater importance than formerly. Physical presence of Christ in the consecrated bread and wine is denied and communion is in both elements. The Supper service is simple and short, consisting mainly in the recital of the biblical account of the institution of the Eucharist with the repetition of those words over the offerings. It is clearly stated that this is a memorial service, so that all notion of sacrifice or real presence may be eliminated.

There is a sedateness in Presbyterian life and worship. It does not favor exuberance, but rather sobriety and simplicity.

Today the question of doctrine is not an urgent one. This may be a reaction to the past when there were sharp controversies among Presbyterians with the consequence that there were splits and divisions. Presbyterians feel quite free to differ from Calvin and the Westminster Confession. They have respect for them, but feel no necessity to adhere to them. Many Presbyterians do not believe that Jesus was in all truth the Son of God, of the same nature and being as God. They can be quite liberal in their interpretation of the Bible. It might be just to say that the great attraction in Presbyterianism is its great stress on freedom. It is perhaps this fact which gives the Presbyterian churches the aspect of a democratic religious federation. It is in every sense a layman's church.

9. THE REFORMED CHURCHES

As we have seen earlier, churches which followed the theology of Calvin were many. There were Calvinist congregations in Switzerland where they were and are the principal Protestant church of the Swiss Confederation. Other Calvinist congregations were formed in Germany, especially along the Rhine. Calvinist congregations were gathered in France and Holland. Some were born in Hungary and Poland.

All these churches called themselves Reformed. They are sister churches of the Presbyterian churches of the British Isles. Yet they do not form one body with the Presbyterians and the reasons are primarily nationalistic.

Three groups of Reformed churches entered into American life. These were the Dutch, German and Hungarian. The few French Reformed chapels in America are mainly for French nationals during their long or short stay in America. Their language is French and their whole spirit is French. The Swiss Reformed who settled in America entered into the Reformed Churches organized by the Dutch or Germans.

New York, of course, was founded by the Dutch. They

brought with them the Dutch Reformed Church of Holland. It was functioning in New York City in 1628, and there were unorganized Dutch Reformed Christians there and along the Hudson River before that date. Congregations multiplied in New York and New Jersey even after the English took the colony in 1664. The Dutch Reformed were instrumental in founding Queen's College (now Rutgers University) at New Brunswick, N. J., where they could train their ministers without sending them to Holland.

Needless to say, the Dutch had little love for England and they were loyal supporters of the American Revolution. After the founding of the Republic, they grew in numbers through the entry of Germans, Swiss, and even English and Scotch. Yet Dutch was the language of most congregations. A solid union was nevertheless established and in 1867 it became the *Reformed Church in America*, affirming no Dutch allegiance. Today it numbers over 200,000 members and its congregations are found everywhere. Though the names of the members are frequently Dutch, yet Americans of all national origins belong to its membership. Except for isolated congregations, the language of the church is always English. Dutch congregations which were not satisfied with the Reformed Church in America formed two other Churches: *Christian Reformed Church* (1857), numbering about 230,000 members, and the *Netherlands Reformed Church* (1907), a small, exclusively Dutch group.

It is strange that the Reformed Church in America does not unite with one or other of the Presbyterian churches. Except for their European histories, there is little to differentiate them. It has been said that the Reformed Church is a "modified Presbyterianism." In doctrine they do not substantially differ. Both believe in salvation by faith alone and see in the Bible the only source of revelation. The Reformed Church does not use the Westminster Confession as the basic expression of its belief. Instead it holds to three continental declarations of doctrine: 1) the *Belgic Confession*, 1561, composed by Guido de Bres (1523–1567), which was declared as orthodox at the Calvinistic Synod at Dort (or Dordrecht) in Holland in 1618–19; 2) the *Canons of Dort*, which were the condemnation of Arminianism at the Dort Synod; 3) the *Heidelberg Catechism*, composed by Ursinus and Olevianus in the second half of the 1500s for the German Calvinists of the Lower Rhine. Today, however, it is not necessary to hold these doctrines with anything like strictness.

In the matter of sacraments, the Reformed hold for two: Baptism and the Lord's Supper. For these they have a prescribed liturgy obligatory on all, though in other services there is great freedom. Babies are baptized to make them adherents to the church of their parents. Real physical presence of Christ in the Eucharist is denied. Reformed morality is sober but not exaggeratedly severe. Moderate use of alcoholic beverages is not condemned.

Concerning the German Reformed we shall speak later. Here, however, we must mention the Hungarian Reformed Church in America. It is not a large church, containing only some 10,000 members. Its history is true to the pattern of most Protestant churches in this country: it owes its existence and its identity to nationalistic causes. Hungarians did not represent any sector of the original community of the United States of America, nor did they form a large part of later immigrations. Yet from 1880 onwards there was an influx of Hungarians into the new world. Of course, most of them were Catholics who either formed their own parishes or joined German parishes already existing. Some Hungarians were Calvinist, or in their terminology, Reformed. By 1904 there were enough to become an organized church and they called themselves the Free Maygar Reformed Church in America. They still kept their ties with the Reformed Church in Hungary. That church, however, urged the Hungarians in America to enter the German Reformed Church in the United States.

As was so common in Protestant churches, the change of status brought about a split. The Hungarians who did not wish to join the Reformed Church in the United States stayed in their own. They changed its name in 1958 and are now called the *Hungarian Reformed Church in America*. Except for the ties which its members feel for their own Hungarian origins, there is nothing which prevents this little church from entering into one of the leading Reformed churches in this country.

The German Reformed in this land have an interesting history and they have already merged with another church and are already members of a new merger. In Germany the Lutheran Evangelicals looked with hostility on Calvinists who were called the Reformed. Yet in the lands along the lower Rhine the Reformed were numerous. There were others elsewhere, especially in the Prussian lands. In Prussia King Friedrich William III, by decree in 1817, made Lutherans and Reformed one in what was called the United Evangelical Church. Actually the Lutherans outnumbered the Reformed in the union and the Calvinist strain was thus weak. The Prussian pattern was adopted in other German lands, but not universally. Unintegrated Reformed churches remained and some of their members came to America in the eighteenth century. Finally in 1863 the Reformed Church in the United States was organized nationally. It was originally German but gradually became English-speaking.

Before this date, in 1840, some German Lutheran ministers wished to organize themselves along the Prussian unionistic lines and called themselves the Evangelical Union, which grew strong enough so that in 1877 it became the German Evangelical Synod of North America. In the Prussian Union Lutherans by reason of numbers had made their Union quite Lutheran. The reverse happened in America. The majority of the Evangelical Synod were Reformed in their tendencies, and the Synod looked less Lutheran than Calvinistic.

The Reformed Church and the Evangelical Synod were so similar that there was no solid reason why they should be distinct. So in 1940 they became one, with the name of *Evangelical and Reformed Church*. Their theological center is the famous Lancaster Theological Seminary, adjoining but not attached to Franklin and Marshall College in Lancaster, Pa.

There is a strong bent in this church towards church unity.

Hence it is not surprising that in 1957 it joined the Congregational Christian Church. This latter church was itself a merger like the Evangelical and Reformed. It was the fusion of the Congregational Church and the so-called Christian churches. The new union will thus bring together what once were four distinct churches and they will take on a somewhat ambitious name: *The United Church of Christ*. The constitutions of this new church have now been drafted and as the historical strain in all the fusing churches is basically Calvinistic it can be treated as a Calvinistic church. In matters of doctrine it will not be too rigid and it will leave much leeway to its members in the matter of belief. It will be run on a presbyterial basis even if this word is not used. It certainly will be a conspicuously layman's church, though there probably will be ample room for liturgy in worship. It will be a church of respectable size, counting about 2,000,000 members.

10. THE CONGREGATIONAL CHURCH

The first English attempt to settle in America took place in 1584. It and others failed. But in 1607 a successfully permanent colony was established in Jamestown, Virginia. This was the beginning of English colonization in the new world, and the religion of this group was that of the Church of England. This fact is frequently overlooked because the story of the Pilgrim Fathers has captured the popular imagination.

These Pilgrim Fathers were not of the Church of England and they landed in Massachusetts in 1620. Their history is impressive because of their stubborn perseverance in their religious beliefs. Elizabeth I accepted the Protestant reform but insisted on religious uniformity. The Church of England, ruled by bishops, was the religion obligatory on all Englishmen. There were, however, those who believed that the Protestant reform, with its two basic doctrines of justification by faith

41

alone and its affirmation that the Bible was the only source of doctrine, demanded a more thorough reform of the Church of England than had been reached in the time of Elizabeth. Some lost patience, and they decided that the Church of England would not reform. So they left it, and they were called Separatists. Others strove for the reform but stayed in the church. Both kinds were called Puritans because they sought for the purity of the Gospel. However, it is clearer to call those who separated from the Church of England, Separatists, and to call the Calvinizing element within the church, Puritans.

The Pilgrim Fathers were companions of a Separatist group in England which was Calvinistic in its beliefs but understood the reform doctrine as an autonomy of the local congregation which was under neither crown nor bishop. They would not worship in the parish churches of the Anglican establishment, and as a result they were persecuted by law. To free themselves from this vexation, some hundreds emigrated to Leyden in Holland. Though they were unmolested there, they were not satisfied. They had no wish to become Dutch and yet they saw that if they stayed in Holland, they would with time cease to be English. Some of the emigrés decided to go to the new lands in the west. They made their arrangements with the Plymouth Company (an English commercial group with a charter to exploit the northern part of English America) and in the ship *Mayflower* they sailed for the West in 1620. They settled at Plymouth in Massachusetts, with great hardships in the beginning.

Puritans within the Church of England also decided to go to America in order to put their ideas in practice. They formed a colonial company with the licence of Charles I, which was called the Massachusetts Bay Colony, settling in 1629 around Boston. These Puritans as a matter of fact were hardly different religiously from the Pilgrims. Neither wanted bishops or synods over the congregations, which were under the Holy Ghost alone acting through the believer's understanding of the Bible. Both groups believed in the necessity of a life of strenuous virtue and simplicity. By 1648 they became one and they called themselves the Congregational Churches. Their theology was strict Calvinism.

These New England Congregationalists were an interesting group. They influenced the history of the United States very much. Yet it is hardly true to say that they understood democracy as the American Constitution conceives it. The Congregationalists believed that they were a people whom God had gathered together to manifest his divine designs. They were therefore God's people, his by covenant. In civil affairs God's people arranged the laws, and no one not of God's people could have a voice. Members of the church had civil power and no one else. The function of civil government was to order public life in accord with the Gospel as understood by the congregations. In this system civil tolerance was out of the question. Non-Christians and Christians of most other denominations were persecuted. Civil government sought out and punished witches. Sobriety and virtue became demands of civil law and the sanctity of the Sabbath (Sunday) was legally imposed. These were the original Blue Laws. As late as 1833 the Congregational Church was the state religion of Massachusetts, and financed by that state.

Although in the beginning the Congregationalists were strict in their Calvinism and accepted the Westminster Confession as a genuine expression of their faith, with time they became more open-minded. Since each congregation was free, no power beyond the majority of the congregation could impose doctrine on its members. The congregation recognized the Bible as its teacher but, of course, it had to interpret it. By the middle of the nineteenth century Congregationalists were not concerned with the Westminster Confession or any other creed. In 1913 in Kansas City they formed a creed which they considered roughly indicative of the faith of most Congregationalists. For them creeds are not tests of belief, but believers' testimony to the faith within them according to the needs of time and place. The man who enters into a Congregational church does not have to profess any set propositions of doctrine. In a word, the Congregationalists reverence the creeds

43

of the past Church but are not held by them. Properly, they are a creedless fellowship of believers.

As a matter of fact they do believe in the sufficiency of the Bible for all doctrine, provided there is freedom of inquiry with the right of private judgment. They baptize children and adults who have not yet been baptized, using the words: "I baptize thee in the name of the Father, and of the Son, and of the Holy Ghost. Amen." Any form of applying the water is valid, but immersion is not usual. Yet baptism is optional.

Worship follows the general evangelical pattern, though there is a growing interest in liturgical service, which is something less than general. Formerly the Congregationalists would only use the Psalms in their singing but now they sing modern hymns as well. Communion service is held occasionally but not too frequently — four to six times a year. There is no belief in Christ's physical presence, and communion is given in both bread and wine. Like Presbyterian service, Congregational worship is simple and severe. Ministers can be either male or female, though most are men.

The minister must belong to the congregation and is chosen by the congregation. He is ordained by ministers of nearby congregations, though in principle the congregation can do its own ordaining, which takes the form of the laying of hands on the candidate.

Much as the Congregationalists stress freedom for the individual and for the congregation, they have another principle which keeps them from being all alone. This is the principle of fellowship. Congregationalist churches enter into union with other Congregational churches, though the union does not impose its will on the congregations. Congregations form an Association with other Congregationalist churches in the region. The Associations (somewhat like Catholic dioceses) unite into the State Conference. Over the State Conferences stands the National Council. To all of these unions the individual congregation sends its delegates, ministers and lay folk. In this way freedom and fellowship balance each other off. The Associations have some indirect control on the congregations, without the congregation losing its own liberty.

The Congregationalists have always favored church unions. In the nineteeenth century they had a union with the Presbyterians, but because it was to their disadvantage they dropped it. In 1931 they merged with the Christian churches (a group which looked very much like Baptists but were quite broad in their theological views and congregational in their church government). They were called Congregational Christian Churches.

This merging church entered into union with the Evangelical and Reformed in 1957. Nor need we think that this will be the last merger. Congregationalists do not consider themselves to be *the* Church but rather congregations of the one Church. They are therefore eager to bring about an ever growing union of all existent churches. They do this on their principle of fellowship. This will not at all destroy the freedom of the congregations, which can erect their own beliefs and worship.

Although Congregationalists were numerous in proportion to the whole population in the early days of the Republic, today they are not so strong. In the merger with the Christian churches, they count about 1,400,000 members. Now that the union with the Evangelical and Reformed Church is completed, there will be over 2,000,000 of them with the title, *United Church of Christ.*

The Congregationalists before the mergers were the wealthiest of all American churches but the expanding union will probably change this fact. They have always been interested in higher education, with a brilliant catalogue of schools: Harvard, Yale, Dartmouth, Williams, Amherst, Oberlin, Carleton, and Pomona.

11. THE ANGLICAN COMMUNION OF CHURCHES

According to the Arthurian legend, Joseph of Arimathea brought the Holy Grail, the chalice which Christ used at the Last Supper, to England. If this were true, the Church of Christ would have been in the British Isles as early as the first century of the Christian era. It is unmistakably true that the Church was in England in the 200s. This church, of course, was in union with the church in Rome. Its members were mainly Romanized Britons who were driven in the sixth century to the southwest of England where they isolated themselves from the invading pagan Anglo-Saxons.

In 597 Pope Gregory the Great sent a group of monks under St. Augustine to plant the church among the English, i. e. the Anglo-Saxons. Augustine's work was successful and he became the first Archbishop of Canterbury, having as colleague the bishop of York. In 668 Pope Vitalian reorganized the English church when he sent Theodore of Tarsus to be Archbishop of Canterbury.

The missionaries whom Pope St. Gregory sent to England were Benedictine monks just as the Pope himself was. They introduced Benedictine monasteries into England, and these became a very important force for learning and holiness.

The English church had to suffer much during the invasions of the heathen Danes during the 800s, but thanks to King Alfred and holy bishops it survived, and in Norman times was strong, becoming the one religion in England and the islands.

England in the Middle Ages was very Catholic indeed. Its schools, shrines, beautiful cathedrals, learned and holy men and women, were glories of the English people.

But the church was not without its troubles, of which the main one was the will of the kings to be masters of both church and state. This tendency came to full flower in the time of Henry VIII. Henry always was and always wanted to be Catholic. He had studied theology and in his writings he opposed

46

Luther, for which Pope Leo X gave him and his successors the title of Defender of the Faith. Henry did not wish to found a new church, but for reasons of power and money he wanted no interference from the Pope of Rome. He made the Parliament declare the King to be the Head of the Church in England and thus he broke the relations of the English church with Rome. He did not, however, tolerate any change in the Catholic doctrine of his church nor did he want radical changes in its worship. In present-day language we would say that Henry put the Church of England in schism, but not in heresy. In other words he separated the Church of England from Rome, but he did not tamper with its Catholic doctrine and piety.

The Protestant reform was powerful and active in this time. Many Englishmen were attracted to it, especially the scholars. After Henry's death, the politicians saw practical benefits in reforming the English church according to the Protestant reform pattern. They ran the government when the boy Edward VI (1537–1553) came to the throne at the age of nine. This reforming policy ended when Mary, Henry's only surviving child by his Spanish wife, Catherine of Aragon, took the throne in 1553. She restored unreformed Catholicism and brought the Church of England into reunion with Rome. She was severe in her program and lost the support of the politicians. She died in 1558 and Elizabeth I, the daughter of Henry's second wife, Anne Boleyn, became queen. Under her rule the Church of England was rebuilt along the lines of the Protestant reformation without, however, accepting all of Protestantism. For one thing, Elizabeth insisted that the bishops under the crown should stay and be the rulers of the churches.

It was in Elizabeth's time that the *Thirty-Nine Articles of Religion* were given their final shape and imposed on all by law (1571). These thirty-nine short statements are derived from Lutheranism and Calvinism but worded in such a way that they stay somewhat vague. For worship the *Book of Common Prayer* in English was made obligatory. This was by Henry and Edward's reforming Archbishop of Canterbury, Thomas

Cranmer. It was a collection derived from the Catholic Office and Mass with some changes to make them fit in with Protestant theology.

To this day the Thirty-Nine Articles and the Book of Common Prayer are the basic books for Anglicans (i.e. English Church members) in their beliefs and services. However, in our time Anglicans do not feel themselves bound to follow these books closely, if at all.

The mind of Elizabeth was to have unified and uniform church life in England. Hence her churchmen and politicians permitted different groups within the church to interpret the Elizabethan reform differently. There was a Catholic-minded sector anxious to retain the notion of tradition and many of the traditionally Catholic positions. These thinkers were ardently in favor of bishops, and needless to say the bishops themselves belonged to this group. On the other hand, there were convinced Calvinist Anglicans, the Puritans, who wished to rid the Church of England of all traces of Catholicism. In between them, there was a large sector which just wanted peace and they were quite satisfied with the ambiguities in the thought and life of the Anglican Church.

As time went on, the English government gave citizens a larger freedom in matters of religion. Those who did not want to belong to the Church of England had the liberty of making up their own congregations. These were and are called Nonconformists or Chapel Folk (because they did not go to parish churches but met in simple and usually small buildings looking like chapels). The Catholics were the last to be accepted, as Parliament passed the Catholic Emancipation Act only in 1829. But to this day the wearer of the crown must be a member of the Church of England and defend Protestantism.

The Church of England was definitely a national church as long as England did not move beyond its boundaries. However, politics, commerce and emigration took England beyond the isles. In this outflow the Church of England moved also but in moving could not remain the Church in England. Scotland had made Presbyterianism the state church and therefore an episcopal church like that in England became the Episcopal Church of Scotland. The British government tried to convert Ireland to the Anglican way of church life. In this they failed but they did produce the Church of Ireland. When the English came to America the Church of England came with them, but after the American Revolution it became the Protestant Episcopal Church. In this way other Anglican churches came into independent being, e.g. the Church of South Africa, the Church of New Zealand, Church of England in Australia and New Zealand, the Anglican Church of the West Indies. These independent churches are not the Church of England, which is tied down to English soil under the direction of the two archbishoprics of Canterbury and York. Yet all of the churches together form the Anglican Communion of Churches and any member of any of them can take communion in any other church of the total federation. The Archbishop of Canterbury is the honorary head of the whole union but he cannot command anything outside of his own diocese. There is periodically a general meeting of bishops from all Anglican churches at Lambeth, London, where the Archbishop of Canterbury has his residence. These meetings, called Lambeth Conferences, do not make laws for the Anglican community but they are the highest voice in the Anglican churches.

The different churches of the Anglican communion are all related to the Church of England, which is the mother church of them all. All likewise have the Book of Common Prayer. Again all have bishops who are the heads of dioceses. Not only do they have bishops, but priests and deacons as well, and these clerics are ordained by bishops through the laying on of hands.

They are also one in another respect: they all practice the principle of comprehension. This means that they tolerate wide variation of belief and worship in their churches, as long as certain formulas — all capable of various interpretations — are accepted. There are Anglicans who believe and worship like Catholics and there are others who seem to be exactly like Presbyterians or Methodists. The churches are satisfied if the communicant admits that the Bible holds somehow what is necessary for salvation; that the Apostles' Creed and the Nicene Creed, sincerely understood by the believer in his way, are adequate formulas of belief; that there are two sacraments, Baptism and the Lord's Supper; that bishops administer the local churches.

What Anglicans lack in preciseness of doctrine they make up for in the dignity of their church services. The wide varieties of belief make for tolerance and courteous treatment of the neighbor. Perhaps the nicest thing about Anglicans is that they have never lost their respect and affection for tradition.

12. THE PROTESTANT EPISCOPAL CHURCH

In the time of the English colonization of America, the New England region was antagonistic to the Church of England. New York was strongly influenced by the Dutch Reformed Church. Pennsylvania lived in terms of toleration and there were many churches there. Maryland was in its beginnings Catholic with toleration for all non-Catholic Christians. The Catholics, however, soon lost control and were deprived of their freedom. The colony was put under the Church of England. The Church of England was also the church of the other southern colonies.

In all this time there never was an Anglican bishop in the new world. All priests of the Church of England working in the colonies had to be ordained in England, and the Anglican Bishop of London was in charge of American church life. The result was that the Church of England was not too lively in the colonies. The American Revolution brought even more opposition to the Anglicans who were considered in the popular mind to be pro-King. Many of the ministers left America to return to England or to go to Canada. But outstanding men of the

Revolution were Anglicans, and George Washington himself was a practising member of that Church.

After the war the Anglicans realized that they had to reorganize. First of all they wanted their own bishops. Samuel Seabury of Connecticut went to England, where his consecration was delayed. He then went to the Episcopal Church of Scotland and was made bishop in 1784. Slowly the new church took shape and new bishops strengthened its ranks. Given the temper of the Americans at the time, the new church strove for democratic forms of government. Nor was this merely a concession to the moment. American Anglicans in their previous history were little inclined to manage their church affairs through the exclusive action of bishops or clergy. There had never been an Anglican bishop in the colonies, not alone because England would send none but mainly because the Americans did not want any.

In a convention held in 1789 the American Anglicans composed a working constitution for their new church. They called it the *Protestant Episcopal Church*, clearly showing that they stood for the Protestant element within Anglicanism. (In the last forty years many Episcopalians have wanted to drop the word Protestant in their title, but too many wish to retain it.) They organized their congregations by states, and these districts gradually became dioceses, each under a bishop. The dioceses of a set region form a province, and the whole church meets in General Convention, held every three years. This convention has two houses: a house of bishops and a house of deputies. The house of deputies includes both ordained pastors of congregations who are priests (usually called rectors) and also laymen. Each diocese sends four priests and four laymen. The two houses act separately but make joint decisions. This convention is the supreme voice of the Protestant Episcopal Church. It elects the Presiding Bishop who is the head of the American church and is equivalent to an archbishop, but his office is not for life. He does not command the whole church but acts for the Convention. The local bishop rules according to the general constitution. Each diocese has a convention

51

each year at which clergy and laity meet with the bishop to regulate church affairs.

There is much lay action in the church. Next to the priest who is parish rector, there are two wardens who are laymen. They take care of the non-spiritual side of parish life. Each parish has a vestry, i.e., a board of trustees who are laymen and act as the officials of the parishioners as owners of the parish property. There are also lay readers who assist in the worship and at times even preach.

The Protestant Episcopal Church has ninety-one dioceses or quasi-dioceses (these last are called missionary districts). The total membership is over 3,000,000. The church is united, though little groups have splintered off. These latter do not use the name of Protestant Episcopal in their titles.

Since the Protestant Episcopal Church works on the principle of comprehension, there is a great variety of belief and worship in the church. The American revision of the Book of Common Prayer is the basic unifying document, and it is usually printed with the thirty-nine articles of religion in the appendix. The three main services are Morning Prayer (substantially Matins and Lauds in the Catholic Office), Evening Prayer (substantially Vespers and Compline in the Catholic Office), and Communion Service (which is a modification of the Catholic Mass). In Anglo-Catholic churches this service is the Catholic Mass, done in English.

There are well defined groups within the Church. Formerly one spoke of three: High Church, Broad Church and Low Church. Today an Anglican bishop, Stephen Neill, thinks it is better to divide the church into five branches: Anglo-Catholic, Higher rather than Lower, Lower rather than Higher, Evangelicals, and Liberals.

The Anglo-Catholics insist that the Protestant Episcopal Church is not at all Protestant but thoroughly Catholic. They usually think of the Catholic Church as made up of three branches: Roman Catholics, Eastern Catholics, and Anglo-Catholics. The beliefs of the Anglo-Catholics, when not completely identical with that of Catholics, come very close to them

indeed. The question of the position of the Pope in the Church
is not explained by all in the same way, though there are a few
who believe that he has jurisdiction over all the Church and
is infallible. Anglo-Catholics have seven sacraments, Catholic
devotions, monks and nuns, and many of their priests are unmarried. The priest's title is Father. Their churches are exactly
like Catholic churches and the Mass is the Catholic Mass in
English. Anglo-Catholics deplore the Protestant reformation
which influenced the history of the Church of England.

Those who are Higher rather than Lower would say that
the Protestant reformation was in general a bad thing, but it
had a few good points which the Church of England wisely
accepted. This group uses much ritual in their services and they
respect ancient traditions. In the matter of belief they are
usually somewhat vague. Those who are Lower rather than
Higher believe that the Protestant reformation was in general
a good thing but it had some bad features. In their services they
will stick to the Prayer Book and their sympathies are Protestant. In matters of doctrine they have ample views.

The Evangelicals want to be thorough Protestants. They
prefer a Calvinistic order of worship and they detest Anglo-
Catholicism and ritualism. These things for the Evangelicals
are Roman Catholicism, and they want the Protestant Episcopal Church to be thoroughly Protestant. For them the Bible
is enough and they have little use for ancient traditions. They
accept their bishops as church officers but not as sacramentally
empowered directors of the Church. They have only two sacraments: Baptism and the Lord's Supper. They do not believe
in the real presence in the Eucharist as the Anglo-Catholics do.
In matters of belief they are not concerned with Tradition.
The Bible is enough.

The Liberals can be found in all of the previous groups.
It is for them a matter of personal preference which type of
worship one uses. Some Liberals are enthusiastically Anglo-
Catholic in their lives of piety, but the traditional doctrines are
all watered down by naturalistic interpretations. They do not
truly believe in the birth of Christ from a Virgin; they do not

really believe that Christ was God of God; they do not hold in the resurrection of the dead; they reject miracles.

Because of these different groups it is quite impossible to say what the general doctrine of the Protestant Episcopal Church is. However, all will say the Apostles' Creed and most will respect the Nicene Creed. Dignity in worship is common to all, and most Episcopal churches are beautiful and in good taste. Today without exception there will be an altar fixed in the sanctuary, which most Episcopalians will call the chancel or presbytery. The altar carries a plain cross and candles, but in Anglo-Catholic churches the altar is not at all different from a Catholic altar.

The Episcopal Church is neither fully Catholic nor fully Protestant. It has elements of both. Its comprehensiveness and respect for tradition make it appealing to many in our land. It can safely be said that the Protestant Episcopal Church is the socially respectable church of America.

13. THE METHODISTS

In 1703, as the fifteenth of nineteen children, John Wesley was born into the household of the Anglican rector of Epworth, England. His mother was a most pious woman and in the rectory atmosphere John was brought up happily and virtuously. He followed the path of his father and maternal grandfather and was ordained priest in the Church of England. In his student days at Oxford he entered a little club founded by his younger brother, Charles, which they called the Holy Club. With methodical diligence the young men studied the Bible and went to weekly communion. The Oxford students called them Methodists, a mildly derisive name which John Wesley himself accepted with time. Instead of taking a parish as his father had done, he wished to preach to a larger audience. His famous words were: "The world is my parish."

Wesley never left the Church of England nor had he in mind the founding of a new church, yet as a matter of fact he did do so. He was a Book of Common Prayer Anglican and his theology was Calvinistic, but according to the manner of Arminius who stood for free will, free grace and free salvation. Wesley did not care too much about doctrine as such but stressed the need of felt remission of sin through faith in Christ. In his own achievement of this feeling he was influenced by the Catholic book, *Imitation of Christ*, the Moravian Brethren, and Luther's preface to the Epistle of St. Paul to the Romans. For Wesley true felt conversion produced a life of holiness and virtue.

His own method of evangelizing, i.e. preaching conversion to crowds gathered anywhere and everywhere, included the formation of little Methodist societies divided into classes, with a class leader in charge of eleven converts. These leaders would report to Wesley. Wesley had been in Georgia for three years as an Anglican priest and he thus knew America. He retained his interest in the new land though he opposed the Revolution. In England the Established Church looked on Wesley and his enterprise with suspicion and he had to use lay preachers to help him in his work. Nor would the Bishop of London ordain any of them. Wesley, a lawful priest of the Church of England, decided after some study that there was no difference between priest and bishop. He then ordained two elders for America and consecrated an Anglican priest, Thomas Coke, to be superintendent of the Methodists across the sea. He also appointed Francis Asbury to be superintendent though Asbury was not in England. He was later consecrated bishop by Dr. Coke.

Wesley had not used the word bishop in the consecration of Coke but translated the Greek term for bishop by another word. In America the Methodists did not follow the reserve of Wesley. They called the superintendents bishops and they considered themselves an Episcopal Church to which they added the name Methodist. It is not clear just what Wesley's own mind was on this development, but there was no way of stopping it.

CHURCHES IN NORTH AMERICA

So the Wesleyan Methodist societies of England became a church in America. This church with its great use of traveling preachers, ordained and lay, made a great impression on the new country. They travelled everywhere and preached conversion with great enthusiasm and passion. As a result they gathered into their own union many Presbyterians, Congregationalists and Anglicans. They have grown to be the second largest denomination in the United States, and one of their churches, the *Methodist Church*, is the largest Protestant church in the land. It numbers something less than 10,000,000 members, and if we count the affiliated youth who have not yet reached full membership status, the total number would not be too far from eleven million. In America only the Catholic Church is larger than this.

The Methodist Church is very efficiently organized. Its structure is clearly expressed in *The Book of Discipline* which the church publishes. This little volume contains a summary of doctrine which John Wesley gave the church along with his General Rules. These are then supplemented by the Constitution formed by the church itself.

We must not forget that John Wesley was an Anglican priest who never left his church. It is then not surprising that he accepted the Thirty-Nine Articles of Anglicanism, though he shortened them to twenty-four, to which the Methodist Church has added three for the American scene.

The Methodist Articles of Religion are Calvinistic in their tone, but the church does not demand a literal acceptance of the expressions. The doctrine of the Nicene Creed is included but nothing is said about that Creed itself. In the service rules the Apostles' Creed is presented, but again there is no insistence on any particular interpretation. Wesley was not concerned with theology and gave his followers full freedom in the matter. However, he did propose the belief in Trinity, the two natures of Christ and the two sacraments, Baptism and the Lord's Supper. Methodists baptize children and also recognize the baptism of other churches. In the administration of the sacrament they use any of the three forms of applying water: sprinkling, pouring or ducking. The words, "I baptize thee in the name of the Father, and of the Son, and of the Holy Ghost," are pronounced.

Communion is not given too often and when it is, both elements are received by the communicant. Unfermented grape juice is used instead of wine. The usual Sunday service is simple and follows the general outline of all evangelical worship. Liturgy has not yet made a deep mark on Methodist services and the usual garb of the minister is the academic gown.

Though Orders is not considered a sacrament, there are orders of clergy. Even to our time there are lay preachers who have not been ordained. But for administering worship, baptism and marriage, ordination is required. Two orders are thus created, the deacons and elders. (Women can receive these ordinations.) There is not much difference in the functions of the two orders. It can be said that a deacon is a second class elder, who in certain circumstances can do all the elder can. Besides deacons and elders, there are two other orders whose members are not ordained but consecrated. These are bishops and deaconesses.

The bishops are very important in the Methodist Church. They have more powers than the bishops in the Protestant Episcopal communion. Yet there is lay participation in the legislation and discipline of the church. There is an ascending scale of agencies for ordering Methodist life. The lowest level is the Church Conference which is the voice of the local congregation. This unit fits into the District Conference which is under the supervision of a superintendent. (The District is like a rural deanery in the Catholic Church.) The District is under the Annual Conference, which is like a diocese and has a bishop at its head. A number of Annual Conferences form a Jurisdiction, and there are six of them in the United States. The church as a whole meets in the General Conference which is in session every fourth year. In all these conferences clergy and laity take part but there is one body, the Council of Bishops, which is composed only of bishops and it is important in the administration of the church. Even at the meetings of the Annual and Jurisdictional conferences, a bishop presides.

Evangelizing, i.e., preaching in order to arouse the experience of faith and conversion, is a great activity of the Methodist Church. It is not surprising, then, that the Methodists are great missionaries. Perhaps their zeal in this matter is something less than what it was in the last century, but it is still very visible.

Wesley made much of holy living. In fact it can be said that for the Methodists Christianity boils down to the feeling of being personally saved by the redeeming Christ, and living up to redemption in a perfect life. That is why doctrine and liturgy are not so pronounced. Wesley was opposed to all use of liquor and this opposition has stayed in the Church to this day (though there are many Methodists who will drink alcoholic beverages in moderation). Gambling is shunned and opposed. Formerly dancing and smoking were banned, but today this is not characteristic of Methodist congregations in general.

Methodists are very anxious to better the life of the civic community and they are active in all forms of social programs. From the time of Wesley, printing has been much used by Methodists and The Methodist Publishing House is the largest church press in the country. (Under the name of Abingdon Press it publishes religious books which are not necessarily Methodist. Its headquarters are in Nashville, Tennessee.)

The Methodists are also interested in the reunion of all Christian churches and they take part in the activities of the National Council of Churches and in the World Council of Churches. In Canada the Methodist Church was the most numerous of the three churches (Presbyterian, Congregationalist and Methodist) which merged to become the *United Church of Canada*.

In summary it can be said that the Methodist Church is an extremely active body because for Methodists action is far more important than passive inwardness.

14. OTHER WESLEYAN CHURCHES

John Wesley produced more churches than the Methodist Church of the United States. There are Wesleyan churches in England and in the lands of the British Commonwealth. Likewise there are Methodist churches in the countries of Europe and elsewhere. However, we wish to consider only the Wesleyan churches in America. As we have seen in the last chapter, the great Wesleyan church in this country is the Methodist Church. But there are others, related to this church in one way or another.

The question of the Negro has affected most Protestant churches of the United States. The majority of these Americans belong to the Protestant community. Racial difference has produced church differences. The Methodist Church has tried its own solution of the problem. It contains six Jurisdictions. Five are set up on strictly regional bases but the sixth was made not because of geographical boundaries but because of the pigmentation of the believers. The sixth Jurisdiction spreads over the entire stretch of the United States and includes all Negro congregations of the church. There is much concern about this arrangement among Methodists and many wish to change the situation by including the members of the Negro Jurisdiction in the regional Jurisdictions which at the present are made up only of white congregations. (Some Negroes as individuals do belong to some of the white churches. Yet this is not a general condition. Few, if any, whites belong to a predominantly Negro congregation.)

This segregation of Negro Methodists from white Methodists is not in principle a matter of white prejudices. Even today many Negro Methodists prefer to be in a church made up entirely by their own people so that the church may satisfy the needs of its communicants according to their customs and inclinations.

The solution of the Negro Jurisdiction within the Methodist Church is not the one chosen by most Methodist Negroes.

They have two large Methodist churches of their own, and six smaller churches. The membership of all these churches would almost reach the figure of 2,500,000.

The largest Negro Methodist church is the *African Methodist Episcopal Church* which goes back to the days of Bishop Francis Asbury, the great pioneer of American Methodism. It has eighteen districts covering the whole country, though its main strength is in the South. It has its own General Conference every four years. It frequently uses its initials, A.M.E., in referring to itself, and includes over a million members. In doctrine and general church organization it does not differ from the Methodist Church.

Another Negro Methodist church even older than the preceding one is the *African Methodist Episcopal Zion Church*. It was formed in 1796 when a group of Negro Methodists belonging to a dominantly white congregation in New York formed their own independent congregation. If we include the youth affiliates of this church, the total membership would come to a million. It subdivides its total church into twelve episcopal areas.

These two churches do not in any way belong to the Methodist Church, but they have friendly relations with it. Their worship and beliefs are substantially the same. The spirited use of congregational hymn singing, common to all Wesleyan churches, is especially noticeable in the Negro churches.

In the nineteenth century the Methodist Church faced inner strains. Slavery was something which Wesley hated but Methodists of the South did not share his feeling. In consequence, southern Methodists broke off from the northern Methodists, so that two churches were formed. Likewise there were Methodists who felt that the episcopal system was not Protestant enough. They formed the Methodist Protestant Church. However, these three churches merged into the single *Methodist Church* in 1939.

There are still Methodist bodies outside of the Methodist

Church which refuse to be episcopal. At the time of the union of the three main churches, one little group continued its own way. It is called the *Southern Methodist Church* but it is so small that it probably will disappear in the near future. There are three or four similar Methodist groups which left the main stream of American Methodism but they are numerically weak and in constant danger of withering away.

However there is one church which does not use the name of Methodist at all and yet is methodistic in its life and worship. This is the *Evangelical United Brethren Church*. The reason why this church is not incorporated into the Methodist Church is the national origin of its believers. American Methodism was English in its beginnings, though this is no longer true for its present existence. Hence in the early days Methodist worship was conducted only in English so that non-English speakers in this country could not take part in Methodist worship.

Yet there were two German ministers working with their compatriots in southern Pennsylvania. They were strongly attracted to the Methodist way of faith. The first of these two men was Philip Otterbein, who was of the Reformed Church in Germany. He came to the United States where the Methodist stress on lived experience of personal assurance of salvation impressed him deeply. He had this experience, and as pastor of an independent German church in Baltimore he led a movement among those who had been lay preachers under his direction to form a new union. In 1800 the movement was organized into a church with the name of the Church of the United Brethren. The doctrine of this group was exactly like Wesleyan Arminianism: God freely saves sinful man who freely accepts this salvation in a personal awareness of its truth; achieved salvation brings with it a life of virtue and perfection. The group was strict in its morality. They opposed slavery, the use of alcohol, and the frivolous use of the Sabbath. They held for two sacraments: Baptism and the Lord's Supper. In church organization they used bishops and general conferences.

This church would have joined the Methodist Church but

there was the question of the use of German in church services. This the Methodists would not permit. Hence the new church was organized as a fully independent communion.

The second German minister was Jacob Albrecht, later anglicized to Albright, who was born in a German community in Pennsylvania. In 1816 he formed a little group which was called the Evangelical Association. This group later called itself the Evangelical Church. It too was Methodist in belief and organization.

In 1946 the two churches merged to become the *Evangelical United Brethren Church*. The church has about 750,000 members. Its main strength is in the eastern part of the United States.

As far as the doctrine and organization of this church are concerned, it is very much like the Methodist Church. (In the early days Albright's church was called Albright Methodists.) There is the same stress on evangelism — preaching to arouse the feeling of personal salvation, to be followed by a life of virtuous perfection. The question of doctrine is secondary and great freedom is given to the believers.

In the structure of the church we have the combination of rule by bishops with democratic decisions of delegates to a general conference held every four years. Of course this church is not bound by the Methodist Book of Discipline.

When we look at the names of the members of this church we note a large number of German names, but it is not restricted to Americans of German origins. The question which comes to mind is why this church does not unite with the Methodist Church. There is no reason of doctrine or organization which is a serious obstacle. Nor is the question of language a difficulty because both churches now speak only English.

The minor Methodist churches are only variations of the Methodist Church. The causes of separation are not too significant. Since all American Protestant churches feel the stirring of the need for reunion, especially the Methodist churches, it is not unreasonable to think that in a near future Methodists will all become one. If this reunion takes place within Methodism alone, the result will not be too important. The numbers of the Methodist Church will become greater, but nothing new or startling would take place within American Methodism itself. The only effect would be that the Methodist denomination and the Methodist Church would become one identical thing.

15. THE BAPTISTS

We have glanced at the American churches and denominations which are related to three strands of the Protestant reformation of the sixteenth century. They were the Lutherans, Calvinists and Anglicans. There was, as we saw, a fourth force in the Protestant reformation. In the sixteenth century they were called Free Spirits or Anabaptists. Today there are but few direct descendants of those groups which existed four centuries ago. However, the Free Spirit idea has taken on forms in America and we must look at them.

The most numerous of all Protestant denominations in the United States is the Baptist fellowship. It is not truly a church nor does it wish to be one. It is strictly a denomination and includes over 21,000,000 believers. This group is hard to describe because it manifests so much variety in its doctrine and worship. An immensely wealthy man like John Rockefeller was a Baptist but most Baptists are far from being rich. There are distinguished Baptist theologians and yet many other Baptists show little interest in scholarship. Some Baptist churches are beautiful buildings, inside and out, while others are rather shabby halls. Everything seems possible within the Baptist denomination.

In spite of these many internal differences, there are certain common traits shared by all Baptists. The common creed of all is that there should be no creeds. By profession Baptist congregations are creedless communities. Yet there is a common faith. If this were to be put in words it would take a form something like this: the Bible alone is the external teacher and the Holy Spirit is the true internal teacher who speaks to every believing soul and to him personally and individually. This principle can lead two ways. For some Baptists the external teacher is decisive and they will accept nothing which is not in the Bible. For others the Inner Voice is decisive and they will be free in their understanding of the Scriptures. Both groups are genuine Baptists, though they may look at each other with something less than enthusiasm.

One commonly reads that Roger Williams (1630–1683) founded the Baptist Church in the United States. It is not so clear that he did, but it is certain that Baptists make much of him and many of his ideas are shared by Baptists in general. He was a most interesting man. Ordained a priest in the Church of England, he came to America where he worked in Massachusetts. Here he had difficulties with the Puritans because he denied that the civil powers had any right to make any laws concerning religion, which must always be a matter of the individual conscience. He and a few companions left Massachusetts and in 1635 founded their own community in Providence, Rhode Island. They opened their own church and practiced baptism for adults only, which was given by immersion. The Williams community gave all dwellers of Rhode Island liberty to follow their own consciences in their religious concerns.

Baptists did not flourish strongly in the days of the colonies but they grew mightily in the nineteenth century. They had a special attraction for the common man because Baptist organization has no human authority which must be recognized. They had no bishops, no synods, no conferences, and no creeds. Every congregation is gathered by covenant which means that they unite voluntarily, always respecting the full freedom of the individual.

There are certain doctrines which are common to Baptists. They believe that the Bible alone is normative for belief, but some are liberal in interpreting the Scriptures and others are very literalistic. All are firm in rejecting any other formulas of faith, though in the past they were willing to consider the Westminster Confession a valid expression of doctrine. They believe in justification by faith in the atoning death of Jesus and they expect faith to be a felt experience. Faith brings with it a life of stern virtue. Above all they defend strenuously the freedom of the believer. No church, no hierarchy can touch the individual's right to his own understanding of the revelation of God which comes to him through God's immediate action on the believer's soul. Hence there is a strong emphasis on the total separation of church and state. In fact in this country we might say that this article of faith is a central preoccupation of Baptists.

In their church structure the Baptists are strong congregationalists with a militant belief in the undifferentiated priesthood of all believers. Each congregation is independent and one enters into it by a kind of covenant. The congregation passes on each candidate and only after the consent of the congregation can the applicant become one of them. At this moment he is as important as any other member and he can direct worship and preach. Actually this does not normally happen because the congregations have their pastors. They also have elders and deacons. But these officials are chosen by the congregation and the choice does not elevate them out of the level of the rest of the community.

Elders and deacons are stewards of the congregation and there is no real difference between the two offices. They assist the pastor and administer the affairs of the church.

The pastor, in order to be chosen for his task as teacher, must have received an inner call from God before he presents himself as a candidate. When questioned, he must affirm that he has felt the Lord calling him to the shepherd's and teacher's mission. In principle the elders and deacons of the congregation which has chosen the pastor could ordain him. However, this today is rare and the pastor or minister will be ordained by Baptist ministers of the vicinity by the laying on of hands.

The pastor is the usual director of religious services, but any one could perform this function. Baptist ministers either will wear no distinctive garb in their church duties or they will wear the academic gown. Vestments are definitely avoided. There are only two sacraments, which Baptists call ordinances. These are Baptism and the Lord's Supper.

The ordinary service is typically evangelical. The center of the worship is the sermon whose purpose should be the renewal of the experience of faith. In consequence there will be a strong emotional tone to it. Although today many Baptist churches have a stationary altar in the front of the building, there are still Baptist churches with nothing but a pulpit in the chancel — the part of the church which Catholics call the sanctuary. In addition to the sermon there are prayers which are said in free form, i.e., they are not written down in any book. Likewise hymns play a large part in the service. This is the outline of the Sunday morning service, but there is usually an evening service as well which does not differ much from the morning worship.

In the administration of Baptism most Baptists practice immersion: that is, the person being baptized is put into a pool and completely covered with water. Children are not baptized because the Baptists insist that Baptism is a sign that the person has had the experience of saving faith involving a decision to follow Christ. Children cannot do that and so they must wait until an appropriate age, which will be sometime after twelve years.

Baptists insist on a virtuous life after Baptism. This will include the shunning of alcoholic drinks and tobacco. Sunday is observed with great sobriety. (In these matters not all Baptists are equally strict.)

The Lord's Supper is celebrated by Baptists with simplicity. If the church has no fixed altar a table is set up at which the minister sits. He says the words of the Bible over the bread and wine. (Many Baptists use unfermented grape juice, and for the convenience of distribution of the liquid small glasses are used.) Deacons bring the bread and wine to the communicants, who are seated in their pews. There is no belief in the physical presence of Christ in the Eucharist. The frequency of Communion Service (which is generally a part of Sunday morning worship) is not the same for all Baptist congregations. Some celebrate as frequently as once a week; others no more than four times a year.

In spite of the fact that each congregation is completely independent, the Baptists encourage fellowship with other Baptists. There is the Baptist World Alliance to which many Baptist churches belong. But this organization has no authority over the congregation. In this country there are a number of Baptist conventions which unite local congregations into a larger unity. The American Baptist Convention (formerly called the Northern Baptist Convention) numbers more than 1,500,000 members. Its member churches are mainly in the North and this union is far more liberal in doctrine and practice than others. The Southern Baptist Convention, with 1,000,000 members, unites the Baptist churches of the South. It is a stricter form of Baptist faith. There are also two large Negro conventions, the National Baptist Convention of America, and the National Baptist Convention of America, Inc. These two conventions unite more than 2,000,000 Negro Baptists.

The Southern Convention does not enter into the ecumenical movements toward church unity but the American Convention of the North is prominent in such work.

16. DISCIPLES OF CHRIST — CHURCHES OF CHRIST

The nineteenth century in America produced many new churches and denominations. Protestant theologians from Europe, especially from England, Scotland and Ireland, came to America to have the freedom to spread ideas which were not acceptable to the European churches. Along the eastern seaboard they ran into the opposition of the established churches but beyond the Appalachian mountains the field was wide open because of the pioneer isolation of the small communities. Here where the traditional churches were weak or absent, the new men called "reformers" won many people to their causes. We have already seen that the creedless Baptists, with their democratic and local organizations, with stress on lived experience of faith in their service, made many converts. Other groups followed their pattern. One such fellowship called itself simply Christians and from this movement two modern churches have come forth: the *Disciples of Christ* and the *Churches of Christ*.

Though many men had leading parts in this movement, yet two, father and son, Thomas (1763–1854) and Alexander Campbell (1788–1866), can be considered the definitive organizers. Both men were Protestant Irishmen, originally Presbyterian, who left that denomination. For a long time their followers were called Campbellites, or even Baptists, but there soon was a separation from the official Baptist communion.

In their church services they followed the example of the Baptists. The Disciples, however, have a distinctive feature in their worship in as much as they celebrate communion every Sunday, though of course they do not believe in the physical presence of Christ in the consecrated elements. Like the Baptists, a congregation of Disciples is fully independent, but the congregations are loosely united in fellowship through local and state conventions. There is also an International Convention of Disciples of Christ which meets every year but has no authority over the congregations.

Church government is like that of the Baptists. There is a minister who is ordained and there are also elders and deacons, the latter being stewards of the local church. All matters of church interest are settled democratically.

From the beginning there were two great convictions of the Disciples. They abhorred denominationalism and sectarianism. They wanted to go back to the unorganized oneness of the New Testament Church. Hence they refused and still refuse to be called a church or a denomination. They are like the Jerusalem or Antioch communities of the Acts of the Apostles, with no other name than Disciples or Christians. They believe in the one universal Church in which all who believe in the Lordship of Christ are members. The Disciples are great promoters of Christian unity and they work faithfully in the ecumenical movement.

The Disciples do not favor creeds and for them there is only one expression of doctrine, the Bible itself. No more is needed. Thomas Campbell coined the Disciples' slogan: Where the Scriptures speak, we speak; where the Scriptures are silent, we are silent. On this basis two different traditions were formed. One group rejected anything not in the Bible while the other considered such things as indifferent, which could be used but never imposed. The Disciples of Christ today follow the more liberal tradition.

In the matter of faith the Disciples are less emotional than Baptists. By faith they understand an intellectual and rational understanding of revelation sealed by a will to live up to it. They do not believe in a lived experience of trust aroused mysteriously by God. In line with this conception of faith, Disciples are usually liberal in their theology. Nor do they think that theology is too important. The one thing which is important is the acceptance of the message of the Lordship of Christ. The rest is secondary. Hence at their communion service any one who wishes to receive is free to do so, no matter what church he belongs to. Yet in the matter of Baptism, in theory they demand total immersion and for adults only. The rite is only a manifestation of the act of faith.

Most Disciples accept the doctrine of the Trinity, but it is not clear what they understand by it. In many cases it means only that there are three names for the wholly unique God. They do not have too clear a notion of the meaning of Christ the Lord in whom all believe. Certainly many do not believe that he is God in the same sense attached to the phrase "God, the creator of heaven and earth." They insist that they reject the Calvinistic doctrine of the total depravity of all born into this world, but by this rejection they probably deny the notion of Original Sin as well.

The Disciples are numerous. In America there are about

2,000,000 of them, if we include baptized and non-baptized adherents. Their strength, as their history would suggest, lies in the midwest and southwest: Illinois, Missouri, Indiana, Ohio, Kentucky and Texas. They founded the highly influential Protestant weekly, *Christian Century*, which — however in accord with Disciples' principle — is no longer an organ of the denomination but is called and really is a non-denominational journal. Its spirit is generally liberal and naturalistic, and these two marks belong to the Disciples as well.

The original movement of the two Campbells lent itself simultaneously to conservatism and liberalism. The Disciples now represent the liberal trend of the original position. But many conservatives also were involved. For them, the slogan "where the Scriptures speak, we speak; where the Scriptures are silent, we are silent" meant purest Bible literalism. For a long time the two branches lived together but in 1906 they silently separated.

As was already pointed out, the followers of the Campbells used only two names. They called themselves either Disciples or Christians. The local congregation took no other name than a church of Christ. Actually these names are confusing because other groups call themselves the Christian Church or Church of Christ. At all events the Disciples still call their congregations *Christian Churches*, with a subtitle, *Disciples of Christ*. Those who separated themselves from them call themselves *Churches of Christ*.

This second fellowship — for it does not want to be a church — is just like the Disciples in structure but in spirit and doctrine it is very conservative. The reason lies in their strong literalism in explaining the Bible and their suspicion of anything which smacks of a priest-class. They also stress a return to the simple religion of the New Testament.

Three points made themselves felt in the evolution of the Churches of Christ. First, they felt that the use of organs and other musical instruments was not proper for church services. The New Testament is silent on this question and therefore a conservative Bible Christian will not accept musical instruments. On this point some congregations were very stubborn, having no fellowship with congregations which used organs.

The second point had to do with the work and title of ministers. In some congregations the minister or pastor exclusively was directing church business. He was also called "Reverend." The more conservative insisted on the direction of congregational affairs by the elders and deacons. The minister was to be only an ordained member of the congregation. Nor was the title "Reverend" to be bestowed on or used by him. As they said, in reference to New Testament simplicity, "Imagine saying 'The Rev. Simon Peter!' "

The third object of suspicion was organized missionary societies and the use of Sunday Schools. These things are not mentioned in the Bible and the conservatives would not tolerate them. Nor would they collaborate with other churches because this would mean that they were themselves a denomination, which they refuse to be.

The Churches of Christ have no unifying organization other than the local congregation. They do have some periodicals. The total membership of the church will be less than but near to 2,000,000. They live principally in the rural areas of Texas, Arkansas and Tennessee. It is hard to give anything like accurate figures for them because their church has no central office, for this would be something contrary to the extreme congregational and independent spirit of the group.

The two churches, for they are such even though they do not wish to be, are the obverse and reverse of one and the same coin.

17. THE MENNONITES

When we were considering the Baptists and Disciples it was mentioned that they were in a spiritual line with the Anabaptists of the sixteenth century Protestant Reform. This is true but it can be misleading. The Baptists and Disciples came to an Anabaptist position not by the influence of their own ancestors but rather in reaction to inherited Calvinism. But there is in our America a set of churches which have historical continuity with the old Anabaptists or Spirituals as they were called. They are named the Mennonites. They are not too numerous, about 150,000 in all. Yet they are a fascinating group by reason of their way of life which cuts them off in greater or less degree from the rest of the population.

During the stormy days of the Protestant Reform, the main Protestant leaders were Luther and Calvin. Yet there were Christians who, with Luther and Calvin, accepted the Scriptures as the sole repository of revelation without reliance on the tradition of the Church but did not accept either Luther's or Calvin's theological explanation of the Bible. They believed in personal guidance by the Spirit and they were far more literal in their understanding of the Scriptures, with a stronger inclination to bring back their own ideas of the simplicity of the early Christian Church. They formed isolated communities which could be found in the area of north Switzerland and its neighboring frontiers, in Holland, and northwest Germany. One man put them on a road to unity and he was an ex-priest of the Catholic Church, whose name was Menno Simons (1496–1561). From him comes the title of the group of churches called Mennonite.

The Mennonites were persecuted in Europe by Protestants and Catholics alike. Notwithstanding, they survived. Among them was an Alsatian, Jacob Ammann (also spelled Ammon, 1644–after 1708), who emphasized the Mennonite trait of shunning the people not of their faith. His disciples are called Amish Mennonites.

Mennonites and Amish came to America about 1700 with the blessing of William Penn, whose own religion was quite like theirs. They settled in eastern Pennsylvania where there was freedom of religion. From this point they later spread west and into Canada. All were German-speaking and this has stamped them in many ways, because they isolated themselves from others and kept their own tongue and customs. The continuous survival and evolution of the German dialect called Pennsylvania Dutch, still in wide use in some Pennsylvania communities, are in no small part the effects of Mennonite insulated traditionalism.

Few as the Mennonites are in numbers, they yet have many divisions. The three main unities are: 1) the *Mennonite Church*, which is a union of the middle-of-the-way Mennonites, neither liberal nor stubbornly conservative. This church holds a meeting once every two years in what is called the General Conference, but the local congregations enjoy great autonomy. There are over 70,000 in this church. 2) The *General Conference Mennonite Church* is a more liberal and modernizing union including some 35,000 believers. This church's strength lies in the west and Canada, and the headquarters of its General Conference are in Newton, Kansas. 3) The *Old Order Amish Mennonite Church* is very conservative. It has no conference and no central organization. Its main strength is in Lancaster County, Pennsylvania, and the church numbers less than 20,000 faithful. This group does not own church edifices and celebrates worship in the private homes of the members.

Mennonite doctrine is substantially the doctrine of the Protestant reformers of the sixteenth century. Yet it has peculiar differences of its own. All Mennonites believe that the Bible and the Bible alone gives us revelation. However, they insist that the Bible does not give its message unless the soul of the reader is filled with the movement of the Holy Spirit. This Inner Light is more important than the printed page, for the letters without the Spirit give no light. The Inner Light is therefore the strong emphasis of Mennonites.

Mennonites in general are not strongly interested in theology. But it can be said that they believe in the God of the Bible in terms of a Trinity of persons. They believe in Jesus Christ as the Son of God, though their doctrine on Christ's divinity is not too clear. They believe that Christ gave unto fallen man a new law and a new way of living, and he sealed his teaching with his death and resurrection. Salvation is thus more

73

an enlightening doctrine than a sacrificial atonement. Those who believe in Christ will follow his law as this is expressed in the Bible, above all in the Sermon of the Mount.

For the Mennonite, behaving as Christ taught is the main endeavor of the Christian. Theologizing about the Lord is not the primary task. Simplicity of life and complete absorption in the brotherhood through love and unity is true Christian service. The invisible Church is made up of all who live in this way. There is too a visible church which is made up of those who seriously follow Christ but this church is identified with the congregation of believers in a given place.

The visible church is organized with three grades of office. There is a bishop (though some Mennonites call him the elder) who is chosen from the ministers and is really no more than the minister highest in dignity and rank. There is either one bishop to one congregation, or one bishop for a number of congregations. He is in no sense a priest and he wears no distinctive garb or vestments. He leads the communion service where there is one. Under the bishop there are one or more ministers, also called teachers. These are the preachers of the community and they are ordained for the task. Lastly there are the deacons, whom some Mennonites call almoners. They supervise the temporal arrangements of church life. (Although most Mennonites now have church-buildings, the stricter Amish still have none, using each other's homes for services.)

The service is a prayer-meeting with a sermon as its high point. Communion service is held only twice a year. The bishop or minister will preside. The words of the Scripture are said over bread and unfermented grape juice. (The Mennonites in the past used and some still use fermented wine.) After the communion comes a characteristically Mennonite practice of washing the feet of the congregation in accord with the command of the Lord. Foot-washing is then followed by a rite in which all of the congregation give each other the kiss of peace.

What distinguishes the Mennonites is their way of following Christ in great simplicity. All without exception believe in non-resistance to evil. Hence they do not use arms nor will they accept posts in army, police or tribunals. By preference they work on the land and are excellent farmers. In clothes they advocate highest simplicity, all using a garb according to the style of four centuries ago. The Amish will wear coats without lapels and no buttons, only hooks-and-eyes. The women do not use hats but bonnets. (In religious services they use a veil.) The men cut their hair in the form of a bob but do not shave. The women do not cut their hair at all. The strictest will not own automobiles for personal conveyance. They ride in horse-and-buggy. Some will go so far as to refuse to install modern bathroom facilities in their houses.

They believe in schooling sufficient to learn to read and write in order to be able to read the Bible and take part in religious services and the current activity of the farm. They do not favor education beyond that. (This is mainly true of the strict Amish. Other Mennonites cultivate learning.) Mennonites are forbidden to marry outside of their own circle, for they must be a people set apart. Avoidance of luxury, hard work, simplicity of manners, and kindliness to the neighbor are the rules of Mennonite life.

In spite of their idiosyncrasies, the Mennonites are highly admired by Americans at large. Their shy and quaint ways are picturesque, nor do the Mennonites in any way annoy their neighbors. They are utterly honest, and models of laboriousness.

A grave problem faces stricter Mennonites like the Amish. They usually have large families but the father cannot supply all his sons with land. Nor can land be easily gotten in the neighborhood. Younger sons and daughters must therefore leave the community, and when they do, they lose the ways of their Amish fellowship. Likewise, any Amish boy or girl who wishes to be educated beyond the level of grammar school will have to leave his home and people. Newer techniques in farming often need a social framework which Mennonism does not provide, thus tending to dissolve the Mennonite way of life. Although some Mennonites have missions, the strict Amish have none. With an alien world about them and closing in on them, how will they be able to survive with all their quaint and picturesque customs?

18. THE QUAKERS, OR FRIENDS

The Mennonites originated on the European continent and are direct descendants of the Anabaptists. But there was a movement like theirs which arose in England in the seventeenth century. Its founder was a shoemaker, George Fox (1624–1691), who as an itinerant preacher formed societies of friends. When a name had to be given to the group, Fox called them exactly what they were, a Society of Friends. However, a judge who tried Fox for blasphemy was admonished by the prisoner to stand in fear and trembling before the judgment of God. The judge ignored the warning and turned the phrase back on Fox, calling him and his followers, Quakers. This name stuck and it is the one by which they are best known, though they themselves still use the name of *Friends* as their official title.

In our time we are so accustomed to the gentleness of Quakers that it comes as a surprise to discover that in their early days they were notorious for a forthright militancy against the English national state and church. They insisted on freedom of worship which in those days was forbidden by law. They refused to take up arms for military service or police duty. They would not recognize any superiority of rank and called any man *thou* instead of the honorific *you*. They would not remove their hats to dignitaries. The clergy of the Church of England they called "a hireling ministry," and Quakers attending Anglican services would heckle the preachers. They would not take oaths. In their own worship they followed none of the patterns known in their age. In their dress they wore plain clothes, ignoring the styles of the moment. In fact their clothes soon became a kind of garb. (The picture on the *Quaker Oats* cereal box shows a Friend in ancient Quaker dress.)

The Quakers were consistently persecuted in England. The American colonies followed the example of the mother country. Quakers who entered into the first colonies were usually whipped, thrown into jail, expelled from the colony or even put to death. Rhode Island, however, was a solitary exception until William Penn, a Quaker, acquired from the crown of England in 1681 the right to establish a colony in what we now know as Pennsylvania. Here at last the Quakers had a home of their own where they would be unmolested.

In the eighteenth century a deep change came over the Quakers. Their militancy disappeared and they developed a quiet comportment in all things. It is from this time on that their gentleness became characteristic of the group.

In a memorable personal experience the founder of the Quakers, George Fox, sensed an illumination within him, informing him that Christ was near to him in his searchings and sufferings. This led Fox to conceive of man as a being in whom there dwelled a divine light. This is the basis of all Quakerism. Quakers admit the validity of the Bible, and they use it. But the important thing is the Inner Light and it is this which they cultivate. The light makes the Bible meaningful; not the other way around. What is more, this light is in all men, although very few bring it to a bright burn. This light is Christ, for he is the light which illuminates every man who comes into the world.

The Light is to be seen and experienced. It is not to be rationalized and changed into a human creed. The Bible is a record of the visions of men guided by the light, and its expressions when achieved under the Inner Light are sufficient for human salvation. In silence and in the union of fellowship the Quaker burnishes this interior lamp and in this way he is in union with God and his Christ.

The light is in all men and this gives all men a divine dignity. Hence all men are honored and loved by the Friends.

Doing good to the neighbor, especially those suffering from misery and oppression, is the great Christian duty.

There are not too many Quakers in the world, something more than 150,000. Of these, 120,000 or more reside in the United States. There have been many divisions among them but the tendency today is to become one church. In the nineteenth century many were influenced by evangelical revivalism and they introduced evangelical forms of worship into their lives. There are still evangelical Quakers who seem to be much like Baptists.

In general, however, Quakers have their own proper worship and church organization. Instead of speaking of a congregation, they speak of a Meeting. Most still call their edifices of worship, meetings. Although strictly they have no clergy, yet each meeting usually has a minister (called the Elder by some). The meeting has two kinds of reunions, one for prayer and the other for business. The business reunion is called the Monthly Meeting: it is the gathering of the members of one congregation or of two or three congregations in the same area. This meeting sends delegates to the Quarterly Meeting, which settles business problems common to a whole area. Over the Quarterly Meeting stands the Yearly Meeting which gathers together delegates from all the local units of a consolidated union of Friends. This would be a diocese in Catholic terms. The Yearly Meeting maintains friendly contact with other communities of Friends who in their totality are the Church.

These various meetings are conducted in a manner which is completely democratic and completely theocratic at the same time. When the question is raised, anyone regardless of age or sex speaks his mind under the guidance of the Inner Light. When all opinions have been expressed, the chairman of the meeting, who has the title of Clerk, gives "the sense of the meeting." No vote is taken and his formulation is accepted. If, however, there is opposition, a time of meditative silence is called and afterwards there will be a new giving of opinions to be ended by the Clerk's declaration of "the sense of the meeting." If this is not satisfactory, the whole question is shelved for another meeting.

Although all Friends are equal, they do have ministers. A minister is a teacher and leader approved for this task by the Yearly Meeting. He presides over worship and in our time he also preaches. Besides the minister, there are elders who are stewards of the congregation. These men are not distinguished in any way from the rest of the believers but they have a function which is distinct.

In morality the Friends are quite strict. They do not gamble nor drink. They will not engage in the liquor traffic, stock market speculation, lottery or gambling enterprises. They do not own theaters, though they may attend shows within the bounds of moderation. They stand for simplicity and avoid all controversies. They allow each Friend to hold his own opinion, even when this is not altogether in harmony with that of the majority. If a Friend drinks moderately, this is tolerated. Even though they do not believe in taking up arms, if an individual Quaker does it, he is not excommunicated. This great toleration comes from the respect for the Inner Light which is in all.

In this country there are nine corporations holding separate Yearly Meetings. Three are important. The Five Years' Meeting of Friends is composed of eleven Yearly Meetings scattered all over the United States. It has a total membership of almost 70,000. Next is the Religious Society of Friends (General Conference) made up of individual Yearly Meetings of the eastern half of the country. It includes some 30,000 members. The third group is not numerous but significant because it is conservative, and loyal to the old ways of the Quakers. It is called the Religious Society of Friends (Conservative) with some 2,000 members. There are no ministers in this union.

In matters of doctrine the Friends are necessarily very tolerant. There is no creed and since the Inner Light is the only true teaching authority, everyone's views are respected. Yet basically the doctrine of the Quakers accepts the God of the

New Testament, the dogma of the Trinity and the kingship of Christ. They all use the Bible and hymns of the general Protestant tradition.

In worship the traditional pattern is that of the Meeting. In a plain hall with no altar the Friends gather. They act only under the direction of the Inner Light. If anyone is moved to speak, he will do so in the form of sermon, confession (called "giving testimony"), or hymn singing. If no one is moved to say anything, the meeting remains in silence for the alloted time of worship and then leaves. Today, however, many meetings use a worship like that of other Protestant churches, with a sermon by the minister and hymns sung by the congregation. The spontaneity of the services is giving way to a formal program prepared in advance.

The Quaker doctrine is highly spiritual because of its basic insistence on the role of the Inner Light. In consequence the Quakers are opposed to material activities in their approach to God. Hence for them Baptism is not a rite using water but only a baptism in the Spirit. Likewise they do not celebrate the Eucharist because true communion for them is internal. Marriage consists in the vows made by bride and groom before the congregation rather than before the minister.

The Friends have been famous for their works of charity. During the War they organized aid for those who were homeless and impoverished. They are interested in refugees and they seek asylum for them. They favor the cause of peace and they preach pacificism. They are not a proselytizing church and their work abroad is rather an opportunity for Christian service than an attempt to make new members.

19. THE PENTECOSTAL CHURCHES

In the last chapters we have looked at the churches which are in line with the fourth strain in the original Protestant Reform, the Spirituals or Anabaptists. We have seen that only the Mennonites are in historical continuity with the original Spiritual movement. The others are later applications of the old Anabaptist principle which insists that the indwelling Spirit in the individual makes the true Christian. Besides the older churches of this tradition, there are new American creations.

In our country we have a large but un-unified number of Christians who make much of the work of the indwelling Spirit, and they insist that the Spirit makes himself visible in external signs. These signs, called "blessings," are manifestations of highly emotional enthusiasm. In their congregations one "gets religion" and it is the "old time religion."

The historical roots of these Christian congregations are in the Revival movement which was so evident in the second half of nineteenth century America. The Revival was also called Evangelism, the Camp Meeting, or simply the Meeting. This movement began under Methodist and Baptist auspices but with time it became independent of those two churches. It always centered about some powerful preacher who was called an evangelist. In our day Billy Graham is the outstanding example, though he conducts his revival in a way much more moderate than was done in the past. He calls his work a Campaign for Christ rather than a Revival.

In the older pattern the Revival was a very emotional affair. It sought for a felt experience of trust in Christ and his atonement for our sins. Lively music and hymns, drum and tambourine beatings, strenuous preaching, confessions of sin and faith, were the characteristics of the Revival meeting. The purpose of most of the preachers was to lead the people to a life of virtue which was called holiness. Holiness frequently was considered to be an extreme puritanism, prohibiting above all the use of alcoholic drinks, dancing, the theatre, stylish dress and vain display.

One of the marks of a Camp Meeting was the presence of the strange physical reactions of the participants. They would undergo the "jerks," which involved the jerking of the head and body with no possible control. Others rolled on the

81

ground. Listeners would shout and scream during the sermon. Not a few would fall to the ground quite senseless. One feature of this heightened emotionalism was the "speaking of tongues." Members of the group would utter words which were derived from no known language or they would pour forth sheer gibberish. This was identified with the speaking of tongues as recorded in the New Testament. Some evangelists were also faith-healers who cured the physical ills of people who attended the meeting.

Today the Revival is not so visible as it was sixty years ago, and when it is held now it usually takes place in a church with far more sobriety of conduct. The large tent used for Revival meetings in the past is hardly seen today. Men like Billy Graham use auditoriums and the meetings are well organized, with careful supervision of the hearers.

Around the beginning of the twentieth century many who were attracted by the emotionalism of the Revival meetings organized themselves into associations in which the Revival pattern of religious service was the normal worship. There are many such associations and they take on different names. In general they are called Churches of God, Assemblies of God, Pentecostal Assemblies, Tabernacles, Four Square Gospel Tabernacles, and other names which are quite picturesque and strange. It is quite impossible to give anything like accurate statistics for all these groups. Anyone can independently start a church of this kind and many of such meeting places are converted stores, the so-called Store-Front churches. From such centers no accurate figures can be collected nor are they interested in giving such statistics.

Yet it has been soberly calculated that there are many more than a million Pentecostals in America. The membership is very fluid because many of the worshipers are members for only a short time before they enter into more sedate churches or drop religion altogether.

In as much as there is a fixed belief in these believers, one can point to a number of tenets usually but not universally professed by the congregations: 1) the native sinfulness of every human being; 2) justification by faith in Christ alone; 3) the divinity of Christ and a Trinity of divine persons, Father, Son and Holy Ghost; 4) the sufficiency of the Bible alone for the achievement of faith; 5) the literal interpretation of the Bible in all its parts as inspired words of God; 6) baptism for the remission of sins, often by total immersion; 7) a second baptism in the Holy Spirit which gives sanctification, i.e. holiness; 8) this second grace is manifested by "speaking in tongues," faith-healing, ecstatic confession, profound emotional experience, physical exhilaration. Pentecostals usually believe in and practice the sacrament of the Lord's Supper, but there is no general norm for the manner or frequency of communion. Many believe in the prompt return of Christ to rule the world a thousand years before the final resurrection.

In moral direction the Pentecostals are vague. They do indeed profess holiness which prohibits not only what all Christians call sin, but also all gambling, drinking, and "worldliness." Yet in practice, a great many of the Pentecostals are hardly strict. In many there is perhaps a latent idea that "unwilling sin" is not held against the sanctified.

There is no prescribed liturgy used in Pentecostal worship. Most of their meeting places have no altar. Store-Front churches have no pews or kneelers. Worshippers sit on chairs or benches. There is a reading stand on which the Bible rests and from which the preacher preaches with much quotation of Bible texts. Lusty hymn-singing is prominent; the use of tambourines or even trumpets is common; the sermon is usually rousing and vivid; confessions of faith by the listeners, in the vernacular or "in tongues," are always in order, and these may take the form of merely shouting "Amen" or "Hallelujah," or of long harangues; rhythmic handclapping and foot-stamping are widely used. In the past Pentecostals were derisively called "Holy Rollers" from the fact that they used to roll or crawl on the floor. Today this is rare. Their services are seldom brief and they may go on for hours. It will all depend on how long the emotion lasts. Night services are very popular.

The heavy emotionalism in Pentecostal religion, and its unconcern for the intellectual content of religious commitment, disturbs many observers of American Pentecostalism. Yet Pentecostal Evangelism has always been a strong element in American religiosity. Every generation has had its picturesque evangelists, not a few of whom were Pentecostal, at least in their behavior. (Most were not really Pentecostal but enthusiastic preachers of holiness.) In the early years of this century Billy Sunday was a popular figure and after his passing, Aimee Semple McPherson captured the attention of the American public. In our time Billy Graham is highly regarded, though he is a Baptist preacher of holiness rather than of Pentecostalism.

The appeal of the Pentecostal Revival in the nineteenth century was strong for the ordinary man of the south, west and mid-west. This man's learning was not high and his life was hard and drab. The great capacity of the Revival for emotional release, especially in terms of its Pentecostal byproducts, made the Revival very attractive. Things have changed today and American secular culture is much richer. It can in most cases give to the men and women of our time all the emotional satisfactions they need.

The class of people who now adhere to Pentecostalism brings out this truth. By and large they are men and women who do not enjoy all the fruits of typical American civilization. Many think that Pentecostalism is mainly a Negro religion. Actually this is not true; there are more whites who practice it than Negroes. In the early days of Italian immigration there were Italian Pentecostal churches, but they are fewer now. Currently we note a large number of Latin-American Pentecostal congregations, though it is also true that in the large Negro districts of our cities Pentecostal churches are very much in evidence.

All of these people have not yet been granted total equality by the general American community. In consequence they are left to their own small group resources for the solution of the problems of life. The close community relationship of a Pentecostal meeting is a comfort; the exhilaration it produces is transforming; the felt belief of being divinely privileged makes up for the social discrimination of which they are victims. The lack of intellectualism is no obstacle precisely because such men and women do not ordinarily engage in intellectual pursuits.

The future of Pentecostalism depends on the survival of oppressed minorities in American society. In Europe Pentecostalism is quite uncommon precisely because culturally oppressed groups are rarer. To the extent that American civilization absorbs all of its people, Pentecostalism will decline. When the Pentecostal rises on the social and economic ladder of the land, he usually joins a more conventional religious group or falls into a tolerant secularism.

20. THE ADVENTISTS

When dealing with the Pentecostals we saw that they could be considered to belong to the Anabaptist strain in the Protestant Reform, but really in every way they are an American creation of recent origin. There are a number of churches of this kind and we shall deal here with some of the more significant ones. The nineteenth century in America showed three great Protestant concerns. The Methodist and Baptist preachers were interested in the moral side of Christian life, and we call the churches whose main concern is strict Christian behavior Holiness, or Perfectionist, Churches. Other churches were interested in a deep experience in religious worship and teaching, and they cultivated emotionalism with strange bodily action as consequents. These are the Pentecostal Churches. There was a third concern in many and this was related to the future coming of Christ. Such believers made much of the teachings of the *Apocalypse*, where it is stated the Christ would come again and rule with the saints for a thousand years (Apoc. 20:1–6). These are Millennial or Adventist Churches. Most are also called Pre-Millennial Churches because they distinguish themselves from those who say that Christ will come *after* the thousand years of peace and justice. The Pre-Millennials believe that he will come *before*, and after the end of the period he will judge all men, saints and sinners.

In all of Christian history we find preoccupation with the second coming of Christ at the end of the world. The first Christians certainly hoped that it would come soon. The Fathers of the Church, i.e., the Catholic theologians of the first seven centuries, were frequently looking for signs of Christ's second advent. In some places and in some times there was a heavy concentration of attention on the question. This was true for some of the Anabaptists in the sixteenth century and it was true again in the United States in the nineteenth century.

Among the Americans caught up in the concern for the second coming of the Lord was a farmer of New York state, William Miller (1772–1849). Although a man of meager education, he was a devoted student of the Bible and he became a Baptist preacher. By a complicated system of Bible interpretation, he foretold that Christ would come on October 22, 1844. Of course, Christ did not come and this was a great disappointment to the Millerites, as Miller's followers were called. Three of them, Joseph Bates, James White, and White's wife, Ellen G. White, reinterpreted the basis of Miller's prophecy by explaining that Christ in 1844 did indeed enter into the Temple to purify it, but it was the Temple in heaven. After this purification, which consisted in an investigation to see which men and women were faithful to divine revelation, Christ would come to the earth to take with him all faithful believers of the past and present into the heavenly kingdom for 1000 years. The date of this coming was not known and the Adventists wisely do not give any dates today. But they insist that it will be soon: any time now.

Mrs. Ellen G. White had much to do with the organizing of the beliefs of the new church which developed from the Millerite movement. She claimed to have the gift of prophecy and her gift is recognized by the Seventh Day Adventists. The

The Adventists

Seventh Day Adventist Church was not formally organized until 1863 but it is today a very vigorous communion, numbering in the United States more than 300,000 baptized members and about an equal number of children in their instruction classes. (Unbaptized children are not considered to be members, and the Adventists do not practise Infant Baptism.) Their work in the mission fields is very impressive and they have missionaries in most of the lands of the earth. Their headquarters are in Takoma Park, Washington, D.C.

The Sabbatarian Adventists (called Sabbatarian because they keep holy the Sabbath, i.e., Saturday) show the influence of many nineteenth century Protestant particularities. First of all, stimulated by the Seventh Day Baptists, they rejected Sunday as the weekly holy day in spite of the fact that almost all Christian churches make Sunday the Christian Sabbath. Adventists insist that Saturday is the day of rest according to the eternal law of Moses which was not repealed by Christ. Secondly, they believe in the nearness of Christ's second advent.

These two tenets characterize Seventh Day Adventist beliefs in a special way. But they have other doctrines which are stressed and these doctrines were in the air of nineteenth century Protestant life. The Adventists are ultraconservative in their understanding of the Bible, which they explain with great literalism. Like all Protestants, they believe in the sufficiency of the Bible alone for the acquisition of God's revelation. Yet they have a Pentecostal element in this belief. They consider prophecy as a constant charism in the church, and they point especially to the prophecies of Ellen G. White. In their conservatism they reject the theory of evolution, and they do not use the scientific method in the interpretation of biblical passages.

There is also a strong tendency to holiness. All Sabbatarian Adventists tithe, i.e., give ten percent of their gross incomes to the church, and give free-will offerings besides. They forbid the use of alcoholic beverages, tobacco and all narcotics. They also counsel vegetarianism but do not make a religious obligation of it. They have dietary laws which are not imposed

87

on believers but do indicate sound rules of health because God, the wise creator of all, has given indications in the scriptures concerning a diet good for the body. The body is a temple of the Holy Ghost and it should be a worthy dwelling for him and should not be defiled with food which would contaminate it. They demand simplicity of dress and sobriety of deportment. They avoid dancing, card-playing, and theatrical spectacles. They will not bear arms in military service but they do enter into the army and navy to serve as medical officers and assistants. They do not call themselves "conscientious objectors" but rather "conscientious co-operators." They engage widely in medicine because they believe that healing is a function of the preaching of the Gospel, but they do not expect it to be charismatic and they willingly and diligently use medical science.

In general their doctrine is like that of the Baptists, and therefore the Adventists are what we have called a holiness church. They have no creed but believe that the Bible is the only valid expression of revealed truth. They believe in the one God of Scripture and they hold for a Trinity of persons in the God-head: Father, Son and Holy Ghost. They hold the strict divinity of Jesus Christ, who was born of a Virgin, and by his sufferings and death atoned for our sins. Their doctrine on immortality is peculiar. Immortality is not for all men, but only for the faithful followers of God's pure revelation. At death all men are in a state of sleep. At the end of time Christ will wake them up and the saints will live in happy immortality and the sinners will be destroyed altogether.

The Adventists have retained two sacraments which they call ordinances. Baptism is given only to those who have made the act of faith and it is given with a single immersion. They celebrate the Lord's Supper periodically (without fermented wine) and practice foot-washing as a preparation for communion. Their service of worship is like that of the Baptists.

Adventist organization is very efficient and looks much like that of the Methodists but they (Adventists) do not call their officials bishops. They do not have a priestly class because they believe in the priesthood of all believers. The local congregation elects its lay elders and deacons. The minister is appointed by the "local conference" which is a union of various congregations in a district. The minister is paid by the conference rather than by the congregation. The local conference, made up by elected delegates from the congregations, is under a "union conference" roughly like a Catholic archdiocesan province. The highest administrative organ is the "general conference" which consists of delegates from Adventist unions from all parts of the world and it meets every four years. To do its work when the conference is not in session a standing Executive Committee is elected.

As has been said, the Adventists are zealous missionaries. In the mission field they found schools of all kinds, hospitals and clinics. They also publish much literature in explanation of their beliefs. Catholics are uncomfortable with these publications because the Adventists have an unkindly view of Catholics. For Adventists the Catholic Church is the great apostasy manifest in the Catholic substitution of Sunday for Saturday as the Lord's Day. For Adventists the papacy is the Beast of the Apocalypse and Catholics are branded with the mark of the Beast.

The Seventh Day Adventists are the most significant Adventist church in our country but there are others as well, though they are smaller and less vital. These other churches are not as a rule sabbatarian. They include the *Advent Christian Church* with some 30,000 members; the *Church of the Abrahamic Faith* with some 15,000 members and adherents; the *Life and Advent Union* with only some 500 members and adherents; the *Primitive Advent Christian Church*, existing only in West Virginia, with some 1200 members and adherents.

All of these churches are the result of the nineteenth century Millerite movement. With the Seventh Day Adventists they are preparing for the second coming of Christ, and they share the Seventh Day Adventist theory on immortality. They differ in other tenets, especially in the matter of Saturday observance.

21. THE MORMONS

The word Mormon, as is so often the case in names for religions, was originally a word of mockery. It was applied to the members of the *Church of Jesus Christ of Latter-day Saints*. However, the members of this church themselves use the word today and the word no longer has a contemptuous meaning. This church is a typically American creation of the nineteenth century with a fascinating history, a perplexing theology and a very impressive social reality. It is simultaneously a holiness, slightly pentecostal, and an adventist Church.

The religious restlessness of nineteenth century America worked on men of very meager schooling but of great confidence in the right of the individual to work out his own schemes of religious truth. It produced a startling variety of sects and denominations. Many have disappeared but a few survived with vibrant vitality. The Church of Jesus Christ of Latter-day Saints is an outstanding example.

In the first quarter of the nineteenth century in America there was great mobility on the part of the inhabitants. New Englanders dissatisfied with life in the east moved westwards. Many such families first settled in western New York. Revivalist preachers toured this area frequently and people were religiously in high ferment. Many of them were not friendly to the established churches, and the strong individualism in them brought forth rather strange religious ideas and practices. One such man was Joseph Smith (1805–1844.) It is easy for scoffers to ridicule the man for some of the things he did but his productivity marks him as a man of genius. He had very little schooling, possessing only the knowledge of the three R's, and yet he was a combination of practical wisdom, great daring and rich imagination. He was clearly a leader of men, with a great confidence in himself which repeated failures could not destroy. As a young man he declared himself a prophet of God. He rejected all the known churches of his day and affirmed that he was called to organize the true church of Christ for his time.

Mormons insist that they are neither Catholic nor Protestant, but the whole spirit of the church is Protestant even though their total doctrines seem strange to Protestants in general.

Smith had many religious experiences which were for him revelations from God. It is on the basis of these revelations that the Mormon Church rests its case. Among these revelations one brought about the discovery of a book engraved on pages of gold. The book according to Smith was written in "reformed Egyptian." It was in 1827 that Smith received the book, when François Champollion in France was still continuing his study of the famous Rosetta Stone. Champollion did not acquire enough knowledge to do adequate translation of Egyptian hieroglyphics until 1832, the year of his death. Needless to say, Smith never claimed to know Egyptian but with the book of Mormon came a pair of glasses with stones in place of lenses. These, Smith said, were the Urim and Thummim. When he looked through them he could translate the book. His translation was published under the title of *The Book of Mormon*. It is the story of a Hebrew family which came to America around 600 B.C. Some of the descendants were faithful to the revelation of God — the Nephites; others were unfaithful and decayed in culture — the Lamanites. Mormon, a Nephite prophet and chronicler, wrote the story of his people and his son Moroni summarised on golden plates the record written by his father.

There are two purposes in the book. First, it explains the origin of the Indians. They were originally apostate Jews who had killed off the faithful Nephites. Secondly, Christ came to the Americas after his ascension into heaven and founded a church perfectly similar to the one he had begun earlier in Palestine. Both churches disappeared by A.D. 385. The true Church of Christ would be established again in the last days, and its capital would be in America.

Smith did not rely exclusively on the doctrines in *The Book of Mormon*. Throughout his life he received revelations. These are now contained substantially in a book called *The Doctrine and Covenants*. In addition, Smith did another book and it is called *The Pearl of Great Price*. It professes to be revelations made to Moses, Abraham and Joseph Smith. The three Smith books and the Bible are the basis of Mormon religious beliefs. Nor are they alone. The president of the church also receives revelations, and in this way revelation continues to grow.

The ideas in Smith's works are very confusing. One can find the notion that all reality, including God and the spirit, are material. It seems that Smith believed in the existence of many gods. The God who is our Father generated us as spirits from eternity. For sin man was thrust into an earthly body. Yet man is immortal and progresses indefinitely, moving from lower planes to higher planes in his progressive existence. Jesus Christ is the First Born of God the Father's children. The Holy Spirit is a true divine person but without any earthly body. The Trinity is thus professed, but it is not clear whether the Trinity is one God in three persons or a trinity of Gods.

Yet all these subtleties are not much studied by modern Mormons. They stick to the Thirteen Articles of Faith which Smith drew up for the Church. This document has a familiar Protestant ring. It expresses faith in the Trinity; an Arminian rejection of the Calvinist doctrine of predestination; the validity of the Primitive Church; the sufficiency of the Bible; the necessity of faith in Christ's atonement for man's salvation; the need of Baptism by immersion; the continuation of revelation; the prompt coming of Christ who will establish the heavenly Jerusalem in America.

What does distinguish Mormons from Protestants in general is their great insistence on the notion of the Church of Christ. Protestant churches do not believe that any one of them is the Church of Christ, but rather that all of these churches belong to the Church of Christ. The Mormons insist that they and they alone are the Church for our time. The Primitive Church in Europe and Asia was the true church but went into apostasy in the fourth century. This was true for the Nephite Church in America. From the fourth century to Smith's time there was no true church. God restored it when he gave to Smith the priestly authority. Real priesthood makes the true church. In Mormonism it has two branches: Aaronic Priesthood and Melchisedech Priesthood. Any male Mormon, if in good standing, can receive all degrees of the priesthood. The Aaronic priesthood has three grades: deacon, teacher, and priest. (Boys of twelve or over become deacons through the laying on of hands by priests of the higher orders.) The Melchisedech Priesthood, which is the higher branch, has five grades: elder, the Seventies, patriarch or evangelist, high priest, and apostle. The Mormon church has bishops but these are men of the high priest rank of the Melchisedech order with the commission to direct a stake (diocese) or ward (parish). There is also a presiding bishop for the whole church.

The priesthood runs the church. The head of the whole church is the president with two counselors. They must all be high priests. There is a senate under the presidency and this is called the council of Twelve Apostles. The church at large does not nominate men to these posts, but it must approve of them.

In matters moral the Mormons are very strict. Polygamy has long ago been dropped. They give tithes to the general church, i.e., ten percent of their income. In addition they finance their own ward which is like a parish church. They may eat meat but they must be moderate in its use. They do not smoke nor drink. They do not take coffee or tea. Most Mormons work much for the church and they receive no financial remuneration for it. The ward bishop, i.e. pastor of the local congregation, receives no salary or stipend. Mormons are great missionaries and young people are expected to give two years to this work with no pay.

They have two kinds of service. One is temple service, and there are throughout the world eight temples. This has liturgy but it is secret — not even all Mormons have the right to enter. Marriages for eternity take place in a temple. There is baptism for the dead in the temple precinct and the higher grades of the Melchisedech priesthood hold meetings here. In the wards are tabernacles, (the latter are like cathedrals, i.e. first churches of a stake, or "diocesan" district). Sunday service is on the pattern of evangelical services in general. There is weekly communion, but the real presence of Christ in the Sacrament is denied and instead of wine water is used.

We have described the Mormon church of Utah, the Church of Jesus Christ of Latter-day Saints. This is the most important of the Mormon churches. There are about a million and a half members and only baptized adults are counted. If we count as adherents those who are not yet baptized, the number will not be far from two million. Besides this church, there are four other Mormon communions who for historic reasons did not and will not unite with the Utah church. One of the dissident groups has some importance. It is the *Reorganized Church of Jesus Christ of Latter-day Saints.* These followers of Joseph Smith elected Smith's son as president rather than Brigham Young, who led the greater part of the Mormons to Utah. This separate Church has its headquarters in Independence, Missouri, and counts something less than 200,000 members and adherents.

22. THE WITNESSES OF JEHOVAH

An American creation in the field of religion is the group called the *Witnesses of Jehovah.* In their short history they have attracted the attention of all the world. Scattered over the earth, there are more than 800,000 of them, and in the United States they number almost 250,000.

They don't claim to be a church. They deny vehemently that they are Catholic or Protestant or Jewish. For them the words, religion and churches, are devilish terms. Their doctrines obviously derive from Protestant backgrounds, but they are quite different from the usual Protestant formulae.

In their beginnings they were called Russellites. This name came from the founder of the group, Charles Taze Russell (1852–1916). Brought up a Presbyterian, he later became a doubting Congregationalist who, under the influence of the Adventists, regained his faith in the Bible.

Though he was never ordained in any church, he was generally called Pastor Russell. He dedicated himself to the study of the Bible and, after 1872, traveled far and wide preaching the prompt coming of Christ.

The Witnesses do not call Russell their founder because they are of the belief that God has raised up witnesses of Jehovah from the beginning of time.

At the death of Russell, leadership in the movement passed to Joseph F. Rutherford (1869–1942). He was a lawyer and the Witnesses always refer to him as Judge Rutherford, though he was never an elected or appointed judge. Because of his close connection with the work of Russell, he became head of the movement at Russell's death in 1916. Rutherford was an active lecturer and his writings form the main expression of Witness doctrine.

The initial name of Russellite did not please either Russell or his followers. Nor did they themselves in Russell's time use their current name of Witnesses. With Russell as president, the Zion's Watch Tower Society was founded in 1884 in Pittsburgh. This society exists today in double form, one incorporated by the laws of Pennsylvania and the other in New York, with the revised name of Watch Tower Bible and Tract Society. Its main offices are in Brooklyn, N. Y., where the activity of all the Witnesses is directed.

The name of this corporation did not lend itself as a label for the Russellites who came to be known as Bible Students, and were incorporated in England as the International Bible Students Association. The name of *Jehovah's Witnesses* was given to the group by Rutherford in 1931. Today the head of the Witnesses, and therefore president of the Watch Tower Bible and Tract Society, is Nathan H. Knorr, an efficient director of the Witnesses but not so colorful a personage as his two predecessors.

The Witnesses are definitely a church preoccupied with the second coming of Christ. It is their major concern. They have no particular doctrine in the matter of morality. Although they counsel abstinence from alcoholic beverages and smoking, they make no law about these things. In general they stand for simplicity of life, but do not spell it out in detail. They are not concerned whether the Lord's day of rest is Saturday or Sunday, though they hold worship on Sundays. As their name indicates, the great Christian task is to give witness to the prompt coming of our Lord and to this mission they dedicate their time and energies.

For the Witnesses doctrine is of supreme importance. The Bible and the Bible alone is the source of all belief. In consequence they are text-quoters. Their interpretation of the Bible is different from that of other Christian bodies, and this difference is for the Witnesses the sign of the worthlessness and Satanic corruption of all other churches.

The Witnesses achieve their understanding of the Scriptures without any reliance on tradition and they take the words literally. According to them, any human being, just by reading the Bible, can find the truth, even though this truth is utterly different from that found by the great body of Christians for 2,000 years.

For the Witnesses, the Bible teaches that there is one God, called in the Hebrew Bible, Jehovah. (Actually there is no such word as Jehovah in the Scriptures. What can be found in the original Hebrew is the word Yahweh, which was badly translated as Jehovah by the Reformers in the sixteenth century. Witnesses know this, but they say that the word Jehovah is now the popular form of Yahweh.)

There is no trinity of persons in Jehovah. The Word was his first creature, and the Holy Spirit is not a person but an aspect of Jehovah's power.

Adam and Eve were human beings created by God and there is no such thing as the biological evolution of man. Adam sinned and, because of it, all men were condemned to die. The Word became Man, Christ Jesus, who by his sinless life crowned with his death, made salvation possible for those who, like him, were loyal to Jehovah and his law.

There is nothing immortal in man; man does not *have* a soul but *is* a living soul. To the faithful witnesses Christ, at his second coming, will give deathless existence here on earth. At death men sleep and they will be finally awakened by Christ. The faithful witnesses who are alive at his coming will not die at all, and the faithful witnesses who have died before his coming will be awakened to live in peace and joy on this earth for a thousand years, when Christ will definitely judge all men, living and dead.

Those who rejected the truth of Jehovah will be utterly destroyed by fire; those loyal to Jehovah will live forever. The return of Christ will be very soon, so that millions now living will never die.

In the beginning Jehovah made the spirit Lucifer head of our world. Lucifer in rebellion tried to make his control independent of God and thus it is that there is constant conflict among men. Lucifer, who is now Satan, has organized mankind in opposition to Jehovah. He uses human political systems, business, and the religions of earth to keep men from doing the will of God. Those who reject Satan and his works are true to Jehovah and they will have nothing to do with human governments, business arrangements and churches.

Hence it is the Witnesses will not swear allegiance to any country or flag. (This tenet has caused the Witnesses much trouble. Hitler hated them hotly and planned to kill them all. Many of them were prisoners in German concentration camps.) Only Jehovah is king and his coming kingdom is the true land of the Witnesses. Because of the Biblical prohibition of drinking blood, the Witnesses will not tolerate blood transfusion.

Because the time is short, the great task of the Witnesses is to tell all men Jehovah's truth. Hence the Witnesses give much of their time to the spreading of the doctrine. This they do by buttonholing people anywhere; in private homes, meetings and conversation. They also diligently sell literature which is printed in vast quantities at the Brooklyn headquarters. It is printed in all languages because the Witnesses go to all lands and peoples.

The divine worship of the Witnesses is more a Bible-study meeting than a religious service. Since Witnesses are against all churches, the Catholic Church above all, they will not call their meeting places churches. They are Kingdom Halls. Such places are either owned by the Witnesses or rented. They are plain rooms with no decoration and no altar. No hymns are sung.

The Bible is studied according to the lessons in their great journal, *The Watchtower*, which has a circulation over 2,000,000, and which the Witnesses peddle with great zeal to all men. The Witnesses also have their own translation of the Bible which they call the New World Bible Translation, containing two parts, Hebrew and Greek Scriptures (Old and New Testament).

The Witnesses take the universal priesthood very literally. They insist that every Witness is a minister, and they claim exemption from military draft on the ground that they are ministers of the Gospel. Where such an argument is not accepted, they refuse to enter military service.

Though there is no clerical hierarchy, the group is centrally directed and controlled. The Brooklyn headquarters under the headship of the president supervises everything. There can only be one doctrine and only one action.

Periodically, international meetings are held at which hundreds of thousands gather to hear the reports of the president and listen to his exhortations, programs and teaching.

The corporation of the Witnesses is financed by free offerings and by the income derived from the sale of literature published. No financial statement is ever given and no salaries are paid to any Witness. Those who give all their time to the work are given lodging, meals, expenses and a nominal sum for personal needs. Those who do not devote themselves entirely to the movement, but yet work in the distribution of literature and oral propaganda, are paid nothing.

The Witnesses use two sacraments because the Bible so dictates, not because these sacraments do anything. Either at the great international or at regional meetings, they hold mass baptisms by immersion. At the annual time of the Passover they celebrate the Memorial Supper. They do not believe in

the real presence of Christ in the Eucharist and they celebrate
it with bread and grape-juice, fermented or unfermented.

23. THE SALVATION ARMY

Another recent church in our midst is the *Salvation Army*. It
was born in England but soon became strong in the United
States. It has novel and picturesque features but it is not a
radical deviation from the Protestantism of the evangelical
English tradition. In fact, it can be considered to be a variant
of Methodism, and it certainly is a holiness church.

The founder of the Salvation Army, William Booth, was
born in England in 1829. At the age of fifteen he underwent
a deep religious experience which led him to do revival preaching. By 1852 he became a regular preacher in an English Methodist Church. He married Catherine Mumford in 1855, and
she was to be his staunch supporter and collaborator throughout her life. In 1861 Booth separated from the Methodists and
became an independent revivalist, preaching in halls, tents and
in the open. All his life he was attracted to the poor, the oppressed, and the needy. For them he established himself in
the slums of London in 1864. At this time Booth had no intention of founding a new church. The existing churches were
satisfactory to him. He was a sincere believer in Wesleyan
theology and simple in his acceptance of the usual evangelical
beliefs in conversion through inner light and a consequent
commitment to service.

A real difficulty faced Booth in his new work with the
victims of London misery. He made converts but soon found
out that they were not wanted as members in the existing
churches. The differences between Booth's people and the
members of the socially proper churches were too great to
permit true fellowship. With his usual simple forthrightness
Booth decided to have his own church. For this purpose he

founded the Christian Mission, which in 1878 became the Salvation Army.

The reason for this name was Booth's conviction that a new form of evangelism was needed for the people with whom he worked. He adopted the basic structure of the British army as the framework of his new enterprise. His evangelists wore military uniforms and took army titles. He paraded the streets with a brass band and conducted his evangelistic services in a rousing military fashion. His first efforts were met with ridicule and even police arrest, but in the course of the years he won the confidence and admiration of all England. Great as was his zeal to convert the men and women of the slums, he saw that nothing could be done to make them capable of religious interest if their living conditions were not changed. He fed them, in consequence, and gave them clothes. He nursed the sick and protected the children and women. Through his begging, social conditions were improved. He did all this along with the preaching of the Gospel. By the end of his life in 1912 his work was solidly rooted, not only in England but in other lands as well. (From 1880 the work was introduced into the United States. It was successfully directed by Booth's daughter, Evangeline, from 1904 to 1934.)

The beliefs of the Salvationists are evangelical, along the lines of Methodism. The Bible is the sole source of revelation, and salvation is through faith alone. They believe in the God of the Bible, who is a trinity of persons, Father, Son, and Holy Ghost. Conversion through an inner experience is the first objective in religious work. It consists in trust in Jesus Christ, the divine Son of God. Conversion is followed by a life of holiness. Alcohol, tobacco and gaming are shunned. Above all, two tasks of the evangelical are stressed: the Gospel must be preached to all men and Christian service to the neighbor must be practiced. There is no great concern for theology or the formulation of doctrine. The sinfulness of man is underlined; the vicarious atonement for sin by Christ in his passion and death are presented; a call is made to a whole-souled trust in him.

45259

Religious worship is conducted on this basis. There are music, hymn singing, Bible reading, free prayer, testimony and preaching. There is no liturgy and none of the sacraments is used, not even Baptism or the Lord's Supper. Marriages are performed but they are not considered to be sacraments. There is no priesthood. Salvationists do not build churches but use halls in their own corps centers of social work.

What gives distinction to the Salvationists is their organization and also the breadth of their social action. Booth used the army idea and army mystique as far as it could be done. All who join the Salvation Army are soldiers. Those who wish to dedicate their whole lives to it become cadets, who are formed in officer training colleges where they usually stay for the period of a year. They then become officers, which is equivalent to ordination. Officers have grades all the way from lieutenant to general. All officers wear uniforms at all times. No distinction is made between the sexes; women have the same titles as men and with them preach and lead services. Officers are usually married and as a rule with other officers of the Army. They receive no salary but are given what is needed for a simple, frugal life.

The whole Army has its headquarters in London. In the different lands national headquarters are set up and territories are lined out, over which commanders are put in charge. Each territory is subdivided into divisions under colonels or majors. The divisions are made of corps. Each corps is directed by a captain and lieutenant. (The corps is what Catholics would call a parish.)

The organization is not democratic in form but strictly military. Commands come from top down, and officers are appointed by the staff and not by the rank and file.

The Salvation Army looks more like a religious order than like a church. The military garb, the life of poverty of the officers, the notion of obedience: all look like the marks of Catholic religious congregations. Even the preaching of the Salvationists does not have as its end the making of Salvation Army recruits. Conversion is sought and there is no objection

101

Lincoln Christian College

if the convert wishes to belong to some other evangelical church. Those who wish to enter into the service of the Army are welcomed, but this is not required. Nor do all recruits have to become officers. They may stay on in their corps as soldiers, doing the ordinary work of the group without abandoning their normal careers. Perhaps the only reason why the Salvation Army became a church was because evangelical churches had no place for religious orders in their organizations.

The social service of the Army is vast and it is extending into new fields constantly. They began with giving food and shelter in their corps halls. This is still done. In these halls religious instruction is given to children. The sick of the neighborhood are visited and nursed. Out-patient clinics and dispensaries are established. Schools and summer camps for women and children are formed. The Army has organized different programs for rehabilitating physically handicapped persons. They likewise do work in prisons and take care of those who return to society after their terms are finished. In World Wars I, II, and the Korean war, the Army directed its own welfare services for soldiers and sailors. All Army services are given to all men, regardless of nationality or creed.

Yet the prime concern of the Army is evangelical religion. Today the organization has many houses and buildings, but they still continue street preaching. They still use the brass band to attract people. Their work is religious, and the welfare services they give are considered as a part of religious action.

In the United States there are more than 5000 commissioned officers and some 250,000 members or soldiers. The work is spread over eighty-six countries, using one hundred and twenty languages. The American national headquarters is in New York.

Two splits took place in the history of the Salvation Army. In 1882, at the beginning of Salvation Army work in America, some Salvationists broke away to do the same work under a more democratic organization. They called themselves the *American Rescue Workers* and they still exist, though their membership today is only about 2000. Their headquarters are in Philadelphia.

The second split came in 1896. The seceding group was led by Ballington Booth, one of the sons of William Booth. This group also exists in our day and is called the *Volunteers of America*, with headquarters in New York City. The organization contains something less than 30,000 members and about 350 officers.

Both the Volunteers and the Rescue Workers are somewhat more conservative than the Salvation Army. Both splinter groups practice Baptism and the Lord's Supper. Because of the smallness of the groups, they are not as conspicuous or as influential as the Salvation Army.

By reason of the charity and good works of these organizations, they have won the respect and good will of the American people. The vast operations of the Salvation Army could not be maintained without the contributions of very many people who are not themselves members of the Army. Americans take pleasure in assisting the Salvationists in their various projects.

24. CHRISTIAN SCIENCE

Another church formed in America during the nineteenth century was Christian Science. Like other religions of American making, Christian Science looks very different from traditional Christianity. Like other nineteenth century creations, Christian Science claims to go back to the true meaning of primitive Christianity which was lost in the other churches.

The formal name of the Christian Scientists is the *Church of Christ, Scientist*. Its founder was a woman, Mary Baker Eddy, who was born in a small town in New Hampshire in the year 1821. Concerning her life much has been written both by Christian Scientists and others. The Committee on Publications of the Church of Christ, Scientist, is on the lookout for all writings on Mrs. Eddy or Christian Science, with the purpose of correcting all such work if it is not in accord with the Church's own view of the matter. The Committee has been able to reduce hostile or critical literature but not to eliminate it altogether. Hence there is no universal agreement on the character of the foundress of the new church.

Some facts, however, are certain. In her youth Mrs. Eddy, who was born Mary Baker, was of weak health, which was a burden to her through many years. Because of it her schooling was very meager, but she read widely all her life. She was three times wedded. Her first husband, George Glover, died within the first year of their marriage. He was the father of Mary's only child, George W. Glover. Her second husband was an itinerant dentist, Daniel Patterson, a man of dubious character whom Mary divorced in 1873. Her third husband was Asa Gilbert Eddy, whom she married when she was fifty-six years old. At his death in 1882, Mary kept his name and remained a widow to her own death in 1910.

In her youth Mary Baker Eddy was a member of the Congregational Church and was always deeply interested in religion. It was the period of transcendentalism in New England, when idealist philosophy was much discussed and studied. Mesmerism, the use of hypnotism according to the theories of Franz Mesmer (1743–1815), was being cultivated in the United States, especially in New England. In this kind of atmosphere Mrs. Eddy discovered the principles of Christian Science in 1866, when she was forty-five years old. She developed her own thinking as the years went on and she used her ideas in order to heal the sick. She taught others how to do the same and in 1881 founded the Massachusetts Metaphysical College in Boston for such instruction. It was discontinued in 1889. In 1875 she published the principal work of her many writings: *Science and Health with Key to the Scriptures,* in which she expresses her own thought on the meaning of the Gospel of Jesus Christ. In 1879 Mary Baker Eddy founded the Church of Christ (Scientist) in Boston but reorganized it completely by forming the First Church of Christ, Scientist, Boston, Mass. in 1892. Her last years were spent in poor health and she died at Chestnut Hill, near Boston, in 1910.

Mrs. Eddy always insisted that her doctrine was derived from a long and careful study of the Bible. She considered herself led by God to be the first in modern times to see what was really taught in the Scriptures. Yet in her *Science and Health* which is the basis of Christian Scientist doctrine there are many things discussed which are very modern. The fundamental tenet of Mary Baker Eddy is that there is no such thing as matter. Anything which is real is spiritual. Whatever exists is either God or the thought of God. From this first principle she drew the important conclusion that there was no such thing as sickness, because sickness supposes matter. Mrs. Eddy admitted readily enough that the *appearance* of sickness was real because the sick person under delusion really thought that he was sick. Christian Scientist healing consists in stimulating the sick person to see that matter and sickness are only appearances, not realities. Sickness then immediately disappears.

Mrs. Eddy did not wish to use hypnotic suggestion in her healing methods. For her the important thing was to see that God, the All, was spirit and that man is made to the image and likeness of God. In God all is harmony, so that sickness, death and sin have no place in God. They are, therefore, nothing. Christian Science is not merely a healing art, but a true religious faith and trust in God. Christian Science is more concerned in overcoming sin than physical disease.

Mrs. Eddy vehemently denied that she was a pantheist, i.e., a believer that there is only one reality in the universe, which reality is God. Yet her writings can easily lead the reader to think that she is advocating pantheism. Actually Christian Scientists have no creed nor did Mrs. Eddy want them to have one. She did explicitly profess the Protestant belief that the Bible was a sufficient guide to eternal life. She certainly believed in God. It is rather clear that she did not believe in a divine personal trinity. She speaks of God the Father, whom she calls Our Father-Mother God, a phrase indicating God as source of all. The Christ is not a person but only the God-principle ever present as the universal ideal truth. Jesus was a man in whom, more than in any other man, the God-principle which is Christ became manifest. Jesus is not the Christ, but rather the Christ was perfectly reflected by Jesus. The Holy Spirit is merely another name for God, but is no person.

Jesus the Christ saved man, but not by his bodily suffering and death. There are no such things in reality. This is precisely what Jesus Christ showed us. By his resurrection he showed us that life is eternal and death is only a seeming. Christ is our redeemer in the sense that he is the way-shower. His salvation is in his teaching.

Christian Science does not believe in sacraments. Biblical Baptism and Holy Communion are pointers to what man needs: new life and oneness with God. These are achieved in the mind, not in material rites. They come in silent prayer rather than in liturgy. Except for preaching love and harmony, Christian Science offers no detailed moral guidance.

There are, of course, no funerals in Christian Science churches. Christian Scientists try to avoid the words "death" and "to die." They speak of "passing on." They hold for marriage, but it is not performed in their churches. They have no priesthood or clergy. In their services there is no liturgy. The worship uses readers who simply read the Bible and Mary Baker Eddy's book. They never preach. Today they also explain a lesson prepared by the First Church of Christ, Scientist, of Boston. Some time is given for silent prayer. A part of the service is also devoted to hymns and to the reading or proclaiming of testimonies to cures performed.

The Church is well organized thanks to the skill of Mary Baker Eddy. She wrote a *Church Manual* which takes care of services and other congregational matters. In a sense, there is only one Christian Science church in the world and it is the First Church of Christ, Scientist, in Boston. All other churches are simply branches of this Mother Church. No problems of doctrine or policy are solved outside of this church and it controls and supervises all the others. It acts through its administrative board, which keeps itself in existence by electing new members when needed.

There are three kinds of officers in the church. There are no pastors. Every congregation needs its two readers, indifferently male or female, who hold their office for five years and are authorized by the First Church of Boston. Every congregation must have in addition to its church a reading room where only Christian Science literature is available for reading and for sale. In co-operation with the reading room, there are Christian Science lectures given by members of a board of lecturers maintained by the First Church in Boston. The striking feature of Christian Science is its corps of Healers. These are all trained by the First Church of Boston and they must have that church's approval. Healing is produced by prayer and readings, at times not in the presence of the invalid. No drugs or physical therapy are allowed. Good Christian Scientists will not use medical doctors or dentists or drugs for any disease; they will only use their own Healers.

The Christian Scientists publish much literature. *The Christian Science Monitor* is a daily paper which has won great esteem because of the solidity and sobriety of its communication of the news. The *Christian Science Journal* is a monthly periodical devoted to the work and thought of Christian Science. There are also journals in foreign languages for non-English-speaking Scientists. Scientists do not conduct general education institutions.

Mary Baker Eddy did not want any census of the members of her church and therefore the church never gives statistics of membership. The group maintains more than 3,200 churches and branches throughout the world. This may bring the membership to the number of 350,000 of whom far more than half reside in the United States. Vagueness of the doctrine, excellent organization, no detailed moral demands, fine church buildings, and an opportunity for quasi-mystical meditation attract well-to-do members of the general community. Observers note that women far outnumber men in Christian Science congregations.

25. BRETHREN CHURCHES

In many churches of the Protestant tradition it is the custom to address fellow-members as brothers and sisters. However, there are Protestant churches which have the word "Brethren" in their official or popular titles. When we considered the Wesleyan churches, we included one which has the name of the Evangelical United Brethren. Here we shall look at other churches which use the name of Brethren but are not in any sense Wesleyan churches.

Perhaps the oldest church with which the word Brethren is connected is the Moravian Church, also called the *Church of the Moravian Brethren*. As the Moravians rightly point out, they existed before any of the Reform churches came into being.

The Moravian Brethren were a result of the movement started by the Catholic priest John Hus (c. 1373–1415). He was condemned to death for heresy at the Council of Constance (1414–18) and was burnt at the stake in 1415. Hus was a man of upright morality and opposed to the Catholic doctrine of authority of popes and bishops. He also appealed to the Bible in his rejection of many Catholic teachings and practices. His disciples, under the name of *Unitas Fratrum*, i.e. United Brethren, in spite of persecution, maintained themselves especially in Bohemia which was the land of Hus. With time they disappeared as an organized group but the more loyal members secretly kept the Hussite spirit and attitude, though externally they belonged to some other church.

At the end of the sixteenth century a movement grew up in Germany called Pietism. The movement stressed interior faith and religiosity, simplicity of life and worship, a closed community but peaceful relations with all men. One of their outstanding representatives was Count Nicholas Zinzendorf (1700–60). He was a faithful Lutheran but he liked the spirit of the Moravians, which was completely pietistic. He invited a group of them to settle on his estate in Saxony in 1722. They

108

were known as the *Boehmerbrueder*, Bohemian Brethren. Zinzendorf made much of preaching the Gospel to the Negro slaves in America, and also to the American Indians. The Brethren shared this persuasion and went to the West Indies and to the American colonies.

The original pattern of church life for the Moravians was a closed social and economic community of believers. The two outstanding congregations in early America were at Bethlehem, Pennsylvania, and at Salem (Winston-Salem), North Carolina. Moravian influence was greatest on German settlers in America because of the German background of the Moravians themselves. The Brothers spread slowly from Pennsylvania through the mid-west and into Canada. They are no longer closed communities, but are congregations scattered in cities and towns. There are about 60,000 of them in the United States and Canada, gathered into some one hundred and fifty congregations.

The Moravians have a *Book of Order* which indicates their faith and worship. They are loyal to the Reform principle, which makes the Bible the only binding rule for faith and morals. They accept, however, The Apostle's Creed as a valid outline of belief. As for the doctrine of Original Sin, they hold it in the sense of the total depravity of historical man: Jesus Christ has saved us from its consequences, and man is saved by faith. Moravians believe in the Trinity, and in the real divinity of Christ, our Savior, who will come again at the end-time. They demand good works of the faithful and charity to all men. They once stressed pacificism but this stress is now gone.

In worship the Moravians hold to two sacraments: Baptism and the Lord's Supper. They baptize children but do not admit them to communion until they have been confirmed at about twelve years of age. Holy Communion is taken six or seven times a year, but there is no altar in their churches, nor do they demand a clear doctrine on the nature of the sacrament. Their worship is evangelical: preaching, hymns and prayers — but they keep the liturgical year with its calendar of feasts, and they have added new feasts to it. They also have

Love Feasts either as independent celebrations or as preparations for the Lord's Supper. The Love Feast consists of taking buns and coffee in a song meeting at which hymns are sung.

In their church structure the Moravians have bishops, presbyters or elders, and deacons. The bishops do not run the church, though they exercise leadership. They ordain the presbyters and have a succession that goes back to the fifteenth century. The church has two provinces, northern and southern. The highest legislative bodies in each province are the synods, held every five years in the north and every three years in the south. When the synod is in recess, business is conducted by a Provincial Elders' Conference. There is also a world organization for Moravians everywhere. It holds a General Synod every ten years and has an executive committee called the General Directory.

So far we have described the Moravian Church in America (*Unitas Fratrum*). There is a small independent group in Texas which is made up of descendants of Czechs. It is not very different from the above named church. The smaller union is called the *Evangelical Unity of the Czech-Moravian Brethren in North America*. They number no more than 3000 members.

Although the Moravian Brethren have the word Brother in their name, when one speaks of the *Church of the Brethren* one thinks of another group. It is a fruit of the German pietist movement of the seventeenth and eighteenth centuries. The original community was called the Church of the Brethren, or Dunkers. The word "Dunker" is from the German word *dunken*, which means to immerse. The Brethren in their baptism immerse the candidate three times into water. This group came to this country in 1719 where they were welcomed by William Penn into Pennsylvania. Their strength even to this day lies mainly in that state. However, divisions took place within the brotherhood and there are now various churches with the name of Brethren or Dunker. The members of the different churches make up about 225,000 in all.

They are sometimes called German Baptists but this does not mean that they are of the same tradition as the American Baptists of whom we have already spoken. The Brethren are holiness Christians, putting a virtuous life as the main demand of the Gospel. The holiness they propose includes pacificism, abstinence from intoxicating drink, a simplicity of life which avoids worldly pleasures and entertainment, a classless community where all are equally brothers and sisters. In doctrine they are creedless, using the Bible alone as the expression of their beliefs. They are very conservative in their understanding of the Scriptures. They believe in the divinity of Christ, the Virgin Birth, the vicarious atonement of Christ for men who are all born in original sin. Christ, the God-Man, will come again to judge the living and the dead.

The Brethren practice what they call ordinances, which are Baptism for those who have made their act of faith. (Infants are not baptized.) They hold Love Feasts like the Moravians. They partake of the Lord's Supper in both elements. As part of this rite they practice foot-washing and likewise give the kiss of peace. They also have confirmation for the young. Interestingly enough, they also anoint their sick somewhat after the fashion of Catholic Extreme Unction.

Their worship is simple and consists in sermons, prayer and hymns. There is no liturgical symbolism. The Brethren have no clergy in the sense of a class different from the rest. The government of the church is in the congregation: every member of any age or sex has his vote. Administration is in the hands of elders, but the officers of worship, called ministers, are elected by ballot by the local congregation. For administrative assistants, deacons are chosen. Although each congregation is independent, they do unite into district unions and each district has an annual conference. The districts themselves are united into regions and the regions meet in a general conference. The largest of the Brethren Churches is the Church of the Brethren with general offices in Elgin, Illinois. This church has well over 200,000 members.

There is a third church which has Brethren in its title. This is the church of the River Brethren. It was formed in the Mennonite country in Pennsylvania at the end of the eighteenth century and its formal title is *Brethren in Christ*. They are not unlike Baptists. The church is small, counting about 7000 members.

A fourth church calling itself the Brethren has no connection with any of the ones already mentioned. This is the church of the *Plymouth Brethren*. The Plymouth Brethren do not claim to be a church but only a fellowship. They do not recognize the name Plymouth Brethren as their true name but use it as a convenience for identification. They began in Plymouth, England about 1827 where Christians of any or no church affiliation met under the leadership of John Darby. (They were therefore called Darbyites.) Their concern was Bible study and prayer. They all felt themselves to be members of the Church which Christ founded but they did not believe themselves to be in any sense that Church exclusively or even particularly. Some of the members of the Plymouth congregation came to the United States at the end of the nineteenth century. Here they spread and became eight different bodies. There is no over-all union of them all.

They are biblical literalists. Conversion to Jesus through faith is for them the sure sign of salvation which then cannot be lost. In their congregations the whole effort is biblical teaching and exhortation. They are eloquent givers of witness and often tell the stories of their conversion. Belief in the priesthood of all Christians eliminates a clerical class. There is no ordained clergy and those who show themselves to be spiritual leaders become ministers of the assembly. They baptize and celebrate the Lord's Supper every Sunday, but there is no liturgy and no altar.

Their great preoccupation is conversion and the new life it infallibly gives. Their concern is biblical affirmation and they quote the Bible at all times. They are missioners and try to preach the Gospel at home and abroad. They are creedless, priestless, unionless and of good, simple lives. They accept the usual fundamentalist teachings: total depravity of fallen man, salvation by faith in Jesus, divinity of Christ, sufficiency of the Bible for faith and knowledge, total rebirth unto everlasting life by the coming of faith. Sincerity is a mark of the Plymouth Brethren but learning is not in general one of their qualities. Scientific interpretation of the Bible they consider false science.

It is hard to give exact statistics for the Plymouth Brethren since the different congregations are not organized in a union. It is calculated that they number some 25,000 in all of the eight bodies of their denomination.

26. OLD CATHOLIC CHURCHES

There are a number of non-oriental churches which are not in union with the Roman Catholic Church and yet do not derive their origins from the Protestant Reformation of the sixteenth century. They are directed by bishops who trace their descent from consecration by bishops whose episcopal power came in unbroken succession from Roman Catholic bishops in the remote or recent past. The general name for them is *Old Catholic*.

There are three Old Catholic groups: the Holland branch with its center in the schismatic bishopric of Utrecht; the German branch founded in Germany, Switzerland, Austria and Czecho-Slovakia after the Vatican Council of 1869–70; the Slav branch now existing principally in the United States and Canada.

The oldest of these churches is the Utrecht church. Utrecht, in the northern Netherlands, was a Catholic diocese founded in 696 with Saint Willibrord as its first bishop. It became an archbishopric in 1560. Among its traditions was its right to elect its own bishops.

In 1579 Holland became an independent commonwealth after a successful revolt under William the Silent (1553–1584)

113

against the Spaniards who had the rule of all the Low Lands. The new Dutch republic was Calvinist in its religious allegiance and Catholics were persecuted. The situation of the archbishopric of Utrecht was most difficult.

There were long vacancies of the archiepiscopal throne. The Dutch Catholic Church in general refused to accept the Pope's right to condemn false doctrine, and the bishops would not sign Pope Clement IX's condemnation of certain doctrines called Jansenist, so named after Cornelius Jansenius, a Belgian theologian of the sixteenth and seventeenth centuries. The result was that there was no true communion between Rome and Utrecht after 1713, putting Utrecht in schism. No Catholic bishop would consecrate a bishop for Utrecht and the see was long vacant.

In 1724 a missionary bishop, Dominique Marie Varlet, with no authorization from Rome, consecrated an archbishop for Utrecht, Cornelius van Steenoven. Rome did not recognize van Steenoven and declared his consecration illegal. The same missionary bishop also consecrated the two successors of Steenoven, both of whom were excommunicated. The second successor of Steenoven was Peter John Miendaerts, and all schismatic bishops of the Utrecht schism derive their episcopal consecration from him.

There has been a Catholic archbishop of Utrecht ever since 1853. The schismatic line also continues and those in communion with the schismatic bishop are called *Old Catholics*.

Frequently the schismatic archbishop and his suffragans (assistants) are called the Jansenist bishops of Holland, but the name is not accurate in our day. The Dutch Old Catholics owe their present name to a union with some Catholics of the nineteenth century who refused to accept the decrees of the Vatican Council in 1870. These Catholics were mainly in Germany and Switzerland.

The German branch of the Old Catholics grew out of a movement which denied the Vatican Council doctrines of the universal and supreme jurisdiction of the Pope along with his infallibility in *ex cathedra* pronouncements. At a meeting in Munich in 1871, the decision was made to organize the Catholics who rejected the Vatican Council.

A bishop was elected in 1873, and he received his consecration from a suffragan of the schismatic Archbishop of Utrecht. National churches were then set up in Germany, Austria and Switzerland. A closer union of all these churches was established at Utrecht in 1889 when the five Old Catholic bishops then in existence met and drew up a statement which indicated the structure and doctrine of the united Old Catholic churches. The statement was called the Declaration of Utrecht.

With time Old Catholic churches were founded beyond the territories of Holland, Germany, Switzerland and Austria. These different churches never grew to any importance with the exception of the Polish National Church in the United States.

Today Old Catholics in Holland come to about 12,000 members with three bishops. The Old Catholics in Germany number about 40,000 with one bishop. In Switzerland the Old Catholics, who call themselves the *Christian Catholic Church,* have about 30,000 members and one bishop. In Austria there are about 40,000 with one bishop. The Old Catholic churches in Poland and Czecho-Slovakia after the Communist revolutions in these countries officially disappeared and nothing can be said about them.

It is in the United States where the bulk of the Old Catholics now exist. Their history is very confusing. At the request of Bishop Hobart Brown of the Protestant Episcopal Church in the diocese of Fond du Lac, Wisconsin, the Swiss Old Catholic Bishop of Switzerland, Edward Herzog, ordained a former Catholic, Joseph Rene Vilatte, to take care of the Old Catholics in America. Vilatte was given a church in Little Sturgeon, Wisconsin, which was under the jurisdiction of the Protestant Episcopal bishop of Fond du Lac. Vilatte was not satisfied with being merely a priest of the Old Catholics. He wanted to be a bishop, but Bishop Grafton, successor of Brown, refused to consecrate him.

115

Vilatte looked elsewhere. The Old Catholic bishops of Europe and the Orthodox bishops refused likewise. He finally received in 1891 a Bishop's consecration from a former Catholic Portuguese who had become a Jacobite bishop of Ceylon, Francis Xavier Alvarez. (Alvarez took the title of Mar Julius I, Archbishop of Ceylon.)

On his return to America Vilatte consecrated several bishops. He considered himself head of the Old Catholics in America, though he was not recognized by the European Old Catholics of the Utrecht union. In 1925 he returned to France and was reconciled to the Roman Catholic Church and died in a French monastery a few years later.

Some Old Catholic churches in America derive from Vilatte. Vilatte's own establishment is called the *American Catholic Church* but today it is a very small body.

Another bishop consecrated by Vilatte was James Lashley. He organized the *American Catholic Church — Archdiocese of New York*. This church includes some 8,000 members.

Vilatte also consecrated a Negro Episcopal priest, George McGuire, who had founded the *African Orthodox Church* in the Harlem area of New York. The present condition of this church is vague. This can also be said of another Negro Old Catholic Church, the *African Orthodox Church of New York*, founded by Bishop Barrow who had been consecrated by Bishop McGuire.

An Old Catholic Church of greater numerical strength is the *North American Old Catholic Church*. It does not derive from Vilatte but from an Englishman, Arnold Harris Mathew, who was a man very like Vilatte and he consecrated many bishops. Mathew's own consecration to the bishopric was by the Old Catholic bishop of Switzerland. Among others, Mathew consecrated Landas Berghes in 1912. Berghes came to America in 1914 to consolidate the Old Catholics in America. Here he consecrated bishops, one of whom was Carmel Carfora, an Italian ex-Catholic priest. Carfora organized the North American Old Catholic Church in 1917. It is in communion with the Syrian Orthodox Church of Beirut and with the Orthodox Patriarchate of Alexandria. It numbers some 25,000 members and has some four or five bishops.

There are other Old Catholic churches but they are very small and their histories are confusing. None of them belongs to the Utrecht union.

But the one large church in communion with the Old Catholic churches of the Utrecht union is the *Polish National Catholic Church of America.* This church was founded by an ex-Catholic priest, Francis Hodur. Hodur was Polish-born and came to the Scranton, Pennsylvania, area to work as a Catholic priest for his Polish compatriots. There was friction among many American Poles and their Irish-American bishop of Scranton. The upshot was that Father Hodur led a number of Polish Catholics into a schism. There were other such schismatic Polish groups in Chicago and Buffalo, New York. Hodur succeeded in uniting all of them and he was elected their bishop.

The Old Catholic bishop of Utrecht consecrated Hodur in 1907. Hodur organized his church and was its leading spirit until his death at Scranton in 1953. This church had a flourishing mission in Poland before the Second World War but it has now collapsed. Hodur's church is in communion with the Lithuanian and Slovak schismatic Catholic groups. The number of members in the Polish National Catholic Church of America is close to 225,000. The church has four dioceses governed by bishops deriving their consecration through Hodur.

All these Old Catholic churches claim to be Catholic in doctrine and practice. They accept the Catholic creeds, sacraments, and customs. Their worship is the Mass which has been somewhat changed to please Anglicans, with whom they are in intercommunion. The language of the Mass is the language spoken by the group — Dutch, German, Polish, English, etc. They do not believe in the infallibility and primacy of jurisdiction of the Pope. They make much of the episcopate and pride themselves on the authentic succession of their bishops. Their clergy are allowed to be married, though in some of the churches this is frowned upon even though permitted by their laws.

With the exception of the Polish National Church, these churches are all weak. Their claim to Catholic doctrine and life is somewhat weakened by the fact that they have changed and go on changing many Catholic doctrines. There is in all of these churches a leakage of members who return to Roman Catholicism.

27. THE UNITARIAN UNIVERSALIST ASSOCIATION

In May of 1960 two American denominations, the Unitarians and the Universalists, voted to merge into a single church called the *Unitarian Universalist Association* with headquarters in Boston. The definitive union has taken effect in 1961. These two churches are of American origin and have an interesting history. Both began in New England, but with time moved over the whole of the United States. Their name alone might be misleading and so we had better see something of their history and spirit.

The word Unitarian originally pointed to the denial that in the Godhead there are three distinct persons. This doctrine in itself is an old one. Arius, a priest of the church of Alexandria, Egypt, proposed this theory back in the early years of the fourth century, but Arius and his teaching were condemned in the Council of Nicea (325). The idea came up again in later times, especially in the sixteenth century. It was taught by a Spaniard, Michael Servetus, who was burnt at the stake by the Calvinists in Geneva, Switzerland, for teaching heresy (1553). Two Italians, uncle and nephew, Laelius and Faustus Sozzini (also Sozini), started the Socinian movement which denied that there was a trinity in God and taught that God was one person only. For this reason the churches founded by Faustus in Poland were called Unitarian, from the Latin word *unus*, which means one. After some early success in Poland and Hungary, Socinian Unitarianism disappeared.

During the seventeenth century in England some individuals, because they could not find the doctrine of the Trinity in Scripture, denied that Jesus was God, although he was sent by the Father who alone is God. No organized denomination was created by such ministers and believers, although individual Unitarian chapels could be found.

In America Unitarianism developed out of New England Congregationalism. It was aided by the preaching and teaching of the great English chemist, Joseph Priestley (1733–1804), an ordained Presbyterian minister who had turned Unitarian. He spent his last years in Pennsylvania, and his writings rather than his personal contact influenced the New Englanders. William Ellery Channing (1780–1842) is usually considered the founder of organized Unitarianism in this country because of his sermon given at the opening of a Unitarian Church in Baltimore in 1819. The American Unitarian Association was born in Boston in 1825. Leading figures in Unitarianism at this time were the essayist and preacher, Ralph Waldo Emerson (1803–1832) and Theodore Parker, minister and preacher (1810–1860).

In the beginning Unitarianism was a hostile reaction to Calvinism and an application of the Protestant principle that nothing was to be demanded for belief which was not found in the Bible. However, by the twentieth century Unitarianism was an affirmation of the full liberty of the Christian in matters of doctrine with a heavy stress on the obligation of the natural mind to construct its own belief.

As a result, the Unitarians believe nothing on authority, whether it be that of the Church or of the Bible or of long-standing tradition. Faith is open to criticism always, and scientific progress is the best norm of criticism. The Unitarians have no creed. Yet it can be said that nothing supernatural is accepted. They reject the notion of three persons in one God; they deny that Jesus Christ is God; they do not believe in Original Sin; they do not hold the Virgin Birth of Christ, nor his physical resurrection, nor Christ's miracles. For Unitarians the man Jesus was one of many great religious leaders. They respect the Bible as an enlightening book, but consider it as purely human, unscientific and full of errors. Many believe that there is no future life after death. Some do not think God is a person.

With so much rejected, in what sense can the Unitarians be called Christian? In the sense that they were formed within the Christian tradition and have their roots in older Christian churches. But they have made an entirely new construction of Christianity. From the general Protestant tradition they have borrowed the principle of freedom in interpreting the Bible. They are also true to the American Protestant emphasis on good behavior and conduct.

They do not believe in sacraments as means of sanctification. Baptism and the Lord's Supper are not condemned, but they look on them as mere rites of no great importance, nor are they necessary for man's salvation, nor for membership in the church. Their worship is very simple and their churches are more like auditoriums than temples. They do not as a rule have altars (but this is not true of all Unitarian churches). Their worship is in terms of preaching and hymns. The minister has no liturgical vestments. At most he will wear an academic gown when preaching and leading worship. The minister, though ordained, is simply a layman. Each congregation chooses its own minister, who in no sense whatever is considered to be a priest. Since the Bible is no authority, sermons are not necessarily biblical and often are lectures on topics of current interest.

Unitarianism is an extreme form of Protestant freedom in the matter of belief. In spite of the fact that Unitarianism had and still has outstanding men and women in its ranks, the church today has only some 110,000 members. Each congregation is independent and makes its own rules. Yet the congregations are in union with the others of the same belief and name. They form regional unions according to city, district and state. All of them together belong to the *American Unitarian Association* which holds a general conference in Boston every year to which all congregations send delegates. This association cannot make laws for the individual congregations. It functions through an Executive Committee of the Board of Directors of the Association. The annual conference elects the board of directors, a president, and a moderator. The president is elected for four years. The moderator of the church is elected for two years. The president and his directors administer the activities of the whole association; the moderator supervises the church life of the member congregations.

A group almost as old as the Unitarians and with a development completely parallel to theirs, is the *Universalist Church of America*. James Relly (c. 1722–1778) was an English Free Church preacher who taught that all men without exception would be saved. A Wesleyan minister, John Murray (1741–1815), was converted to Relly's doctrine. He was chosen as pastor of Relly-ites, i.e. believers in *universal* salvation, in Gloucester, Massachusetts. The first congregation with its church was organized in 1779. A national denomination was founded at a meeting in Philadelphia in 1790, which drew up a declaration of faith as a charter of Universalism. The final statement of faith was drawn up in a general convention in 1935 at Washington, and it is called the Great Avowal.

Originally the Universalists were a reaction against New England Calvinism. They threw over the doctrine of predestination, favoring the ultimate salvation of all men. They rejected the doctrine of Original Sin and the total depravity of man. With time they denied the Trinity and the deity of Jesus Christ. They also moved in the direction of the Unitarians by making each man free to draw up his own beliefs. Many Universalists consider God to be an impersonal force in the material universe. They do not believe that the Bible is a test for Christian belief and they see other religions as being equally valid with Christianity. They make much of the capacity of human nature to bring about a good society, called the Kingdom of God. They believe that religion is a phase of any man's life and it builds up character. It has nothing to do with doctrines or creeds. Such things are chosen by the believer in order to develop character.

In organization they are very like the Unitarians. Every congregation is autonomous in its worship and churchly life. The minister is chosen by the congregation. They have no objection to Baptism and the Lord's Supper, but they do not think such rites are in any way necessary. Divine service is the same as in the Unitarian church: preaching and hymn-singing. There is no sacramental life and the clergy, though ordained, are mere instruments of the congregation for leadership. They have no superiority of any kind. The church is completely democratic.

There is a national organization and also a state organization. The binding union is the national association. Its headquarters are in Boston. It holds an assembly of delegates from the congregations and state unions every two years. There is a president of the national organization elected by the assembly and also a superintendent whose function is like that of the moderator in Unitarianism.

Universalists and Unitarians are so much alike that their final merger was logical. The Universalists will bring some 70,000 members to the Unitarian Universalist Association. The membership of the new merger will be something under 200,000.

28. NON-DENOMINATIONAL GROUPS

The flexibility of Protestantism in our day permits individual Protestants to worship in churches which are not affiliated with the individual's preferred denomination. Likewise, a person may wish to be Protestant without belonging to any particular denomination. These two facts have produced the growing movement of non-denominational or community churches.

Non-Denominational Groups

In smaller towns there will be members of denominations which are not strong enough numerically to maintain churches of their own. Yet their members want to worship and meet others in religious fellowship. Nor do they wish to change their own denominational affiliation. For such people community churches, non-denominational in their structure but doctrinally satisfactory to most Protestants, have arisen. Such a church does not demand that its "parishioners" give up their denominational allegiance, if they have any, or take on a denominational obligation because of their use of the community church.

The community churches are spreading over the country. Some Protestants prefer them to denominational churches because membership in them demands no denominational commitment. Some, but not all, of these community churches have united in non-organic federations.

The National Council of Community Churches is a federation of non-denominational Christian churches. It was founded by Roy Burkhart of the Columbus, Ohio, Community Church. It is hard to say how many persons belong to the more than 200 churches belonging to the union. It is impossible to say what these different churches hold on to in the way of doctrine, because they belong to no denomination. The prevailing doctrine will depend on the minister. It is safe to say that the worship will be along the customary evangelical pattern, with the sermon as the principal part of the service. Occasionally there may be a communion celebration and the minister will administer baptism when it is wanted. (It will not be required for membership.).

In 1930 in Cicero, Illinois, there was formed the *Independent Fundamentalist Churches of America*. Its headquarters are now in Chicago. It is not a church and refuses to be a denomination nor will it accept as a member church any congregation which wishes to maintain its affiliation with a denomination. Although all the congregations are quite independent, to enter into the union they must subscribe to specific fundamentalist doctrines: the inerrancy of the Bible, God's inspiration of the Bible, the Bible as the only source of doctrine, the divinity of Christ, Christ's atonement for all men by his saving death, man's total depravity because of Original Sin, the early return of Christ to judge the living and the dead. The worship is of course strictly evangelical. Some four hundred churches belong to the association and the total membership of the individual churches is about 90,000. The complete doctrinal demands of the individual churches will vary from church to church. This will also be true of their use of the sacraments, which will never be more than Baptism and the Lord's Supper.

A group which attracts much attention is *Moral Re-Armament*. It does not claim to be a church, nor does it wish to be. It has had a varied history with various names for the group. Today it is known everywhere as Moral Re-Armament and is often referred to by its initials MRA. Its first name, which better tells its basic history, was Buchmanism.

The name Buchmanism derives from its founder, Frank N. D. Buchman. He was born in Pennsburg, Pennsylvania in 1878. He died in the August of 1961. Buchman became a Lutheran minister after having completed his course of studies at the Lutheran Seminary in Philadelphia in 1902. In his first pastorate he had difficulties with the congregation's board of trustees. He resigned his pastorate and became a YMCA secretary at Penn State College (now Penn State University). From that institution he moved to Hartford, Connecticut, to be lecturer at the Hartford Seminary. In Hartford he worked with college students in the evangelistic style.

The Seminary and Buchman had their conflicts and in 1922 Buchman decided to evangelize completely on his own. He worked with the students at Princeton University but the University authorities forbade him the use of the campus in 1926. Buchman then went to England to evangelize the students of Oxford and Cambridge. His style of evangelizing received the name of the Oxford Group movement. (The name was unfortunate because it led people to think that it was some-how connected with the great Oxford Movement of the nine-teenth century, with which, of course, it had nothing in common.) The name was changed in the years preceding World War II and it became Moral Re-Armament. It had a great following until the war broke out, in spite of the fact that Buchman had been accused of being a Hitler sympathizer. During the war Moral Re-Armament declined but rose again after the war years. It is quite vibrant in our time. It is impossible to say how many followers MRA now has, but the figures will certainly run into many thousands all over the world.

It must be remembered that Buchman had never wanted to found a church. The Buchmanites retain their affiliation in their own denominations and churches. The movement is strictly non-denominational, or at most, interdenominational. It is a form of evangelism but in a new style. Buchman has appealed especially to the wealthy and to the socially well placed class. Young people are very active in the movement, which is not surprising since Buchman has always made youth-evangelizing one of his prime interests.

What does the Moral Re-Armament group want to do? To change men — the individual, the group and the world. It wants to make them like Christ to the degree that is possible in the human situation. How will this change come about? By confession, surrender, guidance and sharing. These four things will produce the four absolutes: absolute honesty, absolute purity, absolute selflessness, and absolute love.

Confession means a personal declaration of all personal sin. The groupers make much of this. For them unconfessed sin stays in man and works like a hidden cancer in the body. The first thing needed is to bring it out into the open so that it can be removed. On this point the groupers have always met with severe criticism. Although it is not necessary to confess to the whole group, and it is sufficient to confess one's sins to an individual, yet public confession to the group was very prominent in the history of Buchmanism. Individuals would rise and tell all they had done, especially in sexual matters, with great detail. The consequences of such public confession were not always good.

After confession, surrender was possible. Surrender is the old experience of Christ as personal savior. In this experience the person dedicates himself wholly to be like Christ and be one with him in all things.

Guidance means acting according to the almighty will of God. The Buchmanite, alone or in groups, periodically retreats into silence for a short time. In this "quiet time" God speaks to him wordlessly and tells him what to do. This becomes the unquestioned program for the groupers' subsequent action. This is prayer.

Sharing has a double role. One shares one's sins with the group and one also gives witness to the new life experienced in surrender. Every disciple of Buchman dedicates himself to share with men and every Buchmanite is a missionary. They work individually or in "teams."

In the whole movement there is no expressed theology. No doctrine is given and no doctrine is imposed. Much is made of Bible reading but the fruit to be gained is not theory but practice. Implicitly, however, the old evangelist doctrine of personal conversion is being relied on.

The groups often come together in meetings for a day or more. These are prayer and witness meetings which include "quiet times" when God speaks inwardly to the individuals. The gathering is a "house party" in the home of some individual — usually a wealthy individual. There are, however, two great centers for the groups: one is a renovated hotel in Caux near Geneva in Switzerland. This is the international headquarters. The second great center is on Mackinac Island in Michigan.

The groupers are very zealous. The whole institution seems to have at its disposal great funds with which they can command publicity and keep up their centers and "house meetings."

The churches in general are suspicious of the movement.

In 1957, the Papal Congregation of the Holy Office forbade Catholic priests and religious to become members of the organization. Many bishops have forbidden lay Catholics to take any part in group activities. The bishop of Marquette, Michigan, Thomas L. Noa, in whose diocese the MRA center on Mackinac Island is found, has made such a prohibition for all Catholics in his diocese.

29. SPIRITUALISM

What is known today as Spiritualism or Spiritism is really a very ancient form of man's attempt to get beyond the world of our ordinary experience. In the Old Testament we are given a good description of Spiritualism. In the twenty-eighth chapter of the first book of Samuel, Saul's interview with the "witch of Endor" is recorded. Here Saul is put into conversation with the prophet Samuel who had previously died. (In the modern Revised Standard Version of the Bible the word "witch" of older English Bible translations has given way to the more exact word, "medium.")

Yet we must distinguish between Spiritualism as a religion and the scientific investigation of unusual psychic activity. This latter enterprise is also called the study of parapsychology and wishes to understand the structure and causes of the apparent powers in some men for unusual action, not normally shared by people in general.

In this chapter we shall consider Spiritualism as a religion. As was said earlier, Spiritualism can be found in all times and in all cultures. Our interest is to see it as it is practised in a Christian context. The majority of American Spiritualists wish to be Christians.

American Spiritualism took its birth in the late forties of the nineteenth century. On the theoretical side, in 1847, Andrew Jackson Davis published a book with the name of *Na-*

ture's Divine Revelations, in which Spiritualist belief was presented. In 1848 the Fox sisters aroused much curiosity all over the country, especially in the eastern states. They first lived in a "haunted house" in Hydesville, near Rochester, New York. Later they moved to Rochester itself. The girls claimed to be in communication with a spirit through a code of spiritually produced knocks. A code for the understanding of the meaning of the knocks was worked out by the girls and the spirit. From the combination of Davis's writings and the "knockings" of the Fox sisters a movement of Spiritualist activity became widespread. In its beginnings it was not organized and its main activity was seance sessions.

In a seance the central person is the *medium* — usually, but not always, a woman. The medium is the link between the gathering and the spirits of the world beyond. Through the medium the spirits communicate with the participants of the seance.

This can be done in various ways. The most usual way is for the medium to enter into a trance, i.e., a dreamy condition, and through her voice the spirits speak. The theory is that the medium has perceptive powers not to be found in ordinary human beings, or at least she has them in much higher degree. She is in resonance with the vibrations which come through from the spirits on other levels of our universe.

There are other manifestations of the spirit world. Table rappings and table-tippings produced by the spirits are translated as messages. There is spirit-writing on slates, or the medium herself under the influence of the spirits does the writing. The most spectacular phenomenon is the materialization of the spirit. A human form is given to translucent stuff coming out of the medium's body; this stuff is called ectoplasm. The spirits in contact with the medium show their presence in ways which are not directly connected with the actions of the medium. Tables, the medium, and other things are lifted into the air. Bells can be rung. Voices are heard which are not the voice of the medium.

128

With or without the medium, messages can be received from the spirit world by means of the Ouija board and automatic writing. The Ouija board is a wooden tablet with the letters of the alphabet printed or drawn on it. It also has numbers and the words "yes" and "no." (The word Ouija comes from the French *Oui* and the German *Ja*, both words meaning "yes.") On the board there is placed a tiny table with three tiny legs. The operator or operators put their fingers on the little table. It is supposed that a "spiritual" force acting in the operators moves the table (called a planchette) to spell out messages from the spirits. In automatic writing the same thing is done, except that instead of a board the operator himself is moved to write messages on paper.

All these activities of themselves are not necessarily religious. Spiritualism as a religion holds worship services in addition to seance sessions. Such worship will take place either in a church or in a hired hall. An ordained minister conducts the service. The worship follows the pattern of evangelical worship. There will be Bible reading, prayers, hymns and a sermon or lecture. Some Spiritualists even celebrate Communion services. Not all who take part in seances will take part in worship meetings.

Although Spiritualist groups can be formed and maintained without any affiliation with a general association, yet most groups do belong to such organizations. There are three in America: the *International General Assembly of Spiritualists*, which holds an annual convention and has its headquarters in Norfolk, Virginia; the *National Spiritual Alliance of the U.S.A.*, which also has an annual convention at Lake Pleasant, Massachusetts; and the *National Spiritualist Association of Churches*, directed by an annual convention. These associations, allowing much freedom to the member congregations, supervise the licensing of mediums, lecturers, and unordained ministers. They also regulate the activities and training of ordained ministers, who can be male or female. The three associations include in their memberships more than

175,000 Spiritualists. The number of persons not included in these statistics but who independently attend seances rather than worship services may well be twice as many.

The Spiritualist churches have their doctrines. However, except for the belief in the spirit's survival after human death and in the possibility of communicating with such spirits, the other doctrines are not so important. Of course there is a belief in God but it is not spelled out in detail. Some pronouncements of the Spiritualists can be understood in the sense that God is not personal but rather an Infinite Intelligence on which all things rest. But there is no obligation for the Spiritualist to understand it in this way rather than another. Since American Spiritualists are Christian, they also have a doctrine about Jesus Christ. For Spiritualists he was a man and a medium of great power. He was no more divine than anyone else, since all spirits are in union with divinity. But in the case of Jesus, this union was of the highest order. The Bible is understood as a record of the work of distinguished mediums of ancient times who were in communication with the spirit world.

In the matter of morality, Spiritualists consider the Golden Rule to be the basic norm: "Whatsoever ye would that others should do unto you, do ye also unto them." (Matt. 7:12.) These are the words of Jesus in the Sermon on the Mount, but the Spiritualists do not explain the meaning of this command with any detail.

Concerning the cosmos the Spiritualists believe that it is made up of a series of concentric spheres. The lowest sphere is material, in which living human beings have their existence. However, man is made up of three parts. The important part is spirit whereby man is in contact with God. This spirit is carried by a soul and the soul is in a material body. The soul itself is also called the astral body of the spirit. At death, the soul is freed from the body, carrying the spirit into the higher spiritual spheres, of which there are eight. (Jesus is in the highest sphere which is called the Christ sphere.)

The soul in its ascent to the highest sphere progresses in perfection. There is no hell, though there are spheres where impure souls work off their impurity in order to enter into a higher sphere. The process of perfection is constant.

In the spiritual spheres the life of the spirits in their astral bodies is not altogether different from life on earth. In the lowest spiritual spheres the spirits are still very imperfect nor have they purified themselves completely of the sins which marked their existence on earth.

Those Spiritualists who are mainly interested in the seances which give actual conversation with the departed souls, do not preoccupy themselves with this theology. For many reasons they are satisfied with constant contact with the dead. They look for no more.

Spiritualists know that many mediums are frauds who produce their startling phenomena with trickery. They merely insist that there is a kernel of true mediums in the total group. These are important and the frauds will ultimately be detected.

It is hard to say to what degree Spiritualism can be called Christian. It certainly is quite different from the doctrine and practice of the vast majority of Christians for 2000 years. Yet it is also clear that it has a great attraction for many people in our time. In Brazil it is the religion of a large sector of the total population.

30. RELIGIONS FROM THE ORIENT

In Europe, Christianity gradually took over the religious life of all the peoples. By the year 500 nothing was left of the religions of classical Greece and Rome. However, the religions of India and China were hardly touched by Christianity. What is more, in the seventh century a new religion was born in the Near East and it spread into Asia and Africa. It was Islam, the religion of Mohammed. In the Far East the ancient religions continued to live on and they have done so unto our own time.

These religions have come to America. They have not made a deep impression on our people, though we can find little islands in our national life where eastern religions are professed. They are mainly four.

There is a movement today among Negro Americans to accept *Islam*. But it is impossible to give the numbers of American Negro Moslems. The movement is quite strong in the great Negro community of Harlem in New York City. The reason for the attraction of Islam for American Negroes seems to be political rather than religious. Some — hardly very many — Negroes, in their resentment against the Christian churches which have not done much to give Negroes their rights, are looking elsewhere for religious affiliation. Islam has no color bar and some Negroes find its simplicity congenial to their needs. Yet it is true to say that the present trend in some Negro communities toward Islam is caused, not so much because of a religious concern, as by a protest against white injustice which carries with it a distrust of the American white man's religion.

More stable than any Islamic trend among American Negroes today, is *Bahaism*. This religion was founded in the later nineteenth century by a Persian Mohammedan, Bahá'u'lláh, carrying on a movement started by his half brother, Mirzá 'Ali Muhammad, called the Bab (which means Gate). Bahá'u'lláh's son, 'Abdul-Bahá, systematized the ideas of his father and taught the scheme in many lands, including the United States. From Bahá the believers took their name, Bahái, and they have an imposing, very original, nine-sided temple in Wilmette, Illinois, near Chicago. They have a worldwide organization and in America there are some two hundred local assemblies with common headquarters in Wilmette. No actual statistics are given but there are probably between five and ten thousand believers.

The movement is a unity faith. Bahá'u'lláh considered himself to be the twelfth and last prophet in the Moslem tradition. He saw that the one God wishes complete unity of all people, all races, all religions. In Bahái all faiths are considered

132

as true in part. Baháí brings them all together to give man the whole truth. God is the all-pervasive thought in which all things have their being. This truth was variously given by the great prophets: Zoroaster, Moses, Christ and Mohammed. Now it all becomes one in Bahaism. Men must become one family with one language, members of one class and one government. Human unity includes not only the men here below but also those who have died and are alive in God, where they are ever working their way upwards to perfection of love for all things.

This religion is more a religious philosophy than a vital church.

Buddhism is the doctrine of the Indian prince, Siddhartha Gotama, of the sixth century before Christ. He was called the Buddha, which means the Enlightened One. His ideas formed different kinds of religious schemes which were once strong in India but are weak today in that country. However, it spread into China, and from there into Japan, in which two lands it is still flourishing. It is also strong in Ceylon and Burma.

The Japanese brought it to this country and twenty years ago they organized it in imitation of American Christian churches. There is a superintendent bishop over all the churches of the land and he has his headquarters in San Francisco. The officers of the local communities are called ordained clergymen. They have Sunday services and Sunday Schools. The organization includes over fifty churches and a membership of some 20,000 believers, many of whom are not Japanese. Worship is not sacramental and its purpose is to stimulate meditation and to counsel right action.

The basic doctrine of Buddhism is that man can overcome evil and suffering through enlightenment so that he will abandon all selfishness. Passion and desire cause suffering and man must eliminate all desire and so become free. Since man's own actions set up his way of being, he must move out of his present imperfection, called *karma*. This reform may take a long time and it will continue after death when the soul simply moves into another body. Man finally escapes this long chain of imperfection when by meditation he draws away from all desire and thus enters into a state of happiness called *nirvana*. Buddhism is a religion which tries to save man and it says little about God. It stresses virtue, especially compassion for others, and the giving up of things. Buddhists are pacifists who hold poverty, gentleness and chastity in high regard.

There is a monastic form of Buddhism called *Zen*, which is practiced in Japan. It has attracted the attention of many of today's intellectuals. Zen, however, is being studied more as a philosophy than as a religion.

Two other forms of religion with roots in India have found their homes in America. The older is called *Theosophy*. Theosophists consider their doctrine to be a philosophy rather than a religion. It would probably be wisest to say that it is a religious philosophy rather than a church. American Theosophy was brought to this land by Madame Helena Petrovna Blavatsky (1831–1891), a Russian noblewoman who was a world traveler. She reached America in 1873 where with Col. H. D. Olcott, an American, she founded the Theosophical Society to promote the brotherhood of all men, to study the great religious teachers of all the world, and to investigate the secret powers in man and nature. She left for India in 1879. At her death in 1891, the leadership of her society went to another colorful person, Annie Besant (1847–1933,) an Englishwoman, who became a Hindu and discovered the new incarnation of God, an Indian named Krishnamurti, who later renounced his messiahship. Under William P. Judge the society in America made itself independent of the India group in 1891. It has its own headquarters in Wheaton, Illinois, under the title of *The Theosophical Society in America*. There are a few thousand members. Since this group is not really a church, there are no true religious services of worship, though meetings with lectures are held. Besides this society, there are other (less numerous) theosophist groups.

The main points of belief of this group can be given in the following scheme. The soul has proceeded from God who is the universal spiritual base of all reality. The soul is moving toward this God. However, when in the material body, it loses its purity through sin and ignorance. This is *karma* just as we saw it with the Buddhists. It is a state of man produced by man's own deeds. Man must, therefore, purify himself, though a long series of deaths and rebirths may be required. Along with the spiritual enlightenment taught by *mahatmas* (in the mother language of India, Sanskrit, this word means a wise man of great spiritual soul), Yoga — a way of purifying the soul by mental and bodily exercises — is also taught. The theosophist pursues enlightenment and practices the exercises of the yogis. The end term will be reached in nirvana, the state of sinless rest in the spirit of the divine basis of all things.

American theosophy is a mixture of ideas borrowed chiefly from India, but also from elsewhere. The theosophist sees in Moses, Christ, Socrates and other sages, the incarnation of the divine principle. None is unique. All have something to teach us. There will be more yet to come. All are mahatmas. All, then, must be studied.

There is another society based on Hindu ideas of religion, and it is directed by men from India. This is the *Vedanta Society*. It was organized in the United States by an Indian, Swami Abhedananda, in 1893, as part of the mission work of the Ramakrishna Mission headed by Swami Vivekananda in India. The headquarters of the American Society are in New York, and the Society has eleven branches with some thousand members.

The word *swami* is Hindu and means master or high teacher. It is a title and not a name. The heads of the Vedanta Society have this title and are called Swami, just as we call our college teachers doctors or professors. The Vedanta doctrine is completely Indian though directed toward American conditions. It is not strictly a religion but rather a philosophy which can act as the foundation and stimulus for religion. It is derived from the study of the Vedas, which are the Sacred Books of ancient India. The Upanishads, a late section of the Vedas,

135

are especially studied. The goal which the Vedantists pursue is the knowledge of the nature of all things. This they wish to harmonize with the findings of modern science. They are respectful of all religions, believing that all are partial grasps on spiritual reality. They believe in the essential goodness and virtue of the individual human spirit, and the swamis give instructions whereby man can control his own destiny and achieve spiritual perfection.

All the Asiatic religions described in this chapter fascinate many people of our country, but because they look somewhat strange to the average man only few Americans really belong to these schools of thought. (Most are women.)

31. JUDAISM

There is another flourishing religious denomination in America which comes from the Near East. We rarely think of it as oriental because it is the mother faith of Christianity which we all consider to be Western. This religion is the faith of the Jews.

Americans in general have confused ideas about the Jewish community. Jews are not a national group. It is of course true that the Republic of Israel is a nation but it contains only a minority of all the Jews of the world. American Jews are and want to be Americans. They are not Israeli. French Jews are French; English Jews are English. Jews are Jews not because of their religion but because they form a people which has common traditions and a long history as a recognizable historical unity. Jews are not a race. There is no one blood in them all. Jews have intermarried with representatives of all races.

There is no one Jewish religion. Actually in this country we can speak of at least four different Jewish faiths. All four have much in common but they are yet different and distinct. There are many Jews who are not religious at all and they belong to no religious association. Yet the different Jewish churches, called synagogues, will accept a man into their fellowship as long as he is a member of the Jewish people. Those who are outside of the people can also be accepted by a Jewish church, but this is a true conversion and by conversion the non-Jewish person, or gentile, becomes a member of the Jewish people. The synagogues are connected with the people, but not all the Jewish people are connected with the synagogues. A Jew even if he has no religion still belongs to the people. He can belong to a non-Jewish religion and still be of the people. He ceases to be Jew only when he cuts himself off from the community and identifies himself completely with a non-Jewish cultural group.

In the century before the destruction of the Temple in Jerusalem there was no one set of Jewish beliefs. There were many. As the New Testament points out, there were Pharisees and Sadducees. Besides these, there were the Essenes. The majority of the people did not belong to any of these three groups. But all used the same Temple. For ordinary worship services there were synagogues in the towns and cities, but these were not all of the same theology. The sign of religious unity was then the great Temple where all worshipped from time to time. Those Jews who lived far away from Palestine went to the Temple rarely, or never. When the Temple was destroyed by the Romans, only the synagogues were left as religious centers, but their function was local and not international. They were structured congregationally and the Aaronic priesthood had no function in these gatherings except to give the final blessing. Rabbis, who are scholars of the Jewish religious tradition, supervised the meetings, worship and community life. The priests disappeared as an organized class. It must be remembered that a rabbi is not a priest, though a priest (any male Jew with the name of Cohen) can be a rabbi if he has made the proper studies and has been accepted by a rabbinical union.

There are about seven million Jews in the United States today. Some five million in different degrees have connections with synagogues. The synagogues are grouped into four unities. The largest unit is the group of *Orthodox* congregations.

Orthodoxy demands belief in the teachings of what Christians call the Old Testament. Orthodox Jews also observe the ancient traditions as they are handed down in a collection of ancient rabbinical writings called the Talmud. The dietary laws and the ancient customs in the observance of Sabbath (Saturday) and of the traditional holidays are honored. Orthodox Jews will not work on Saturday (which begins on Friday afternoon at sun-down and ends on Saturday afternoon at sundown). They will not eat pork in any form; no shell fish; no meat slaughtered without the supervision of a rabbi or official appointed for the purpose. The dietary laws are many and very detailed. Food allowed and prepared according to the dietary laws is called *kosher*, which in Hebrew means clean.

Service in the synagogue consists of prayers, chanting of psalms, readings of the Old Testament Scriptures, the rabbi's explanation of the Scripture, and a final blessing of the rabbi or of a priest (Cohen) if one be present. Except for the rabbi's explanation in English, all the rest is in Hebrew. Besides Sabbath service, which is not obligatory for women ever, nor even strictly so for men, there are annual holidays of great moment. The New Year celebrations, Rosh Hashana and Yom Kippur (in early Autumn), and the Passover meal called *seder* (around the time of the Christian Easter) are especially venerated. Orthodox males will have their heads covered in all religious activity, which includes daily meals. (For this purpose they will wear a little skull cap called *yarmalke*. Some Orthodox Jews will wear it almost always.)

The fundamental moral law of all Jews is the table of the Ten Commandments as given to Moses by God. Detailed explanation of the Law is given by the rabbis according to the traditions of the Talmud. All Jews are agreed that Jesus of Nazareth is not the Messiah, the great prophet whom the Orthodox Jews are still awaiting. Concerning the nature of Messiah, modern Jews are not in agreement. The older Orthodox think that Messiah will be a human person. Younger ones are not so sure, many believing that the people of Israel as a people is the Messiah of the Lord.

138

The *Reformed* Jews are quite different from the Orthodox. In general the Reformed call their houses of worship temples, a word that the Orthodox usually (but not always) restrict to the non-existent Temple of Jerusalem. The Reformed consider Jewish religion to be a moral code and a way of life. They are not interested in doctrine or theology. They wish to adapt Judaism to modern conditions, and they do not consider the traditional ways as binding on the contemporary Jew. The Reformed do not, on principle, observe the dietary laws, though in fact they may do so voluntarily at certain times. Hence they are not concerned about kosher food and have no feeling against the eating of pork. Likewise the Reformed do not insist on the circumcision of Jewish males, although the Orthodox do so. In worship service, the Reformed use organs and instrumental music. They use English rather than Hebrew, and the rabbi does not restrict himself to the mere explanation of the Scriptures. He preaches just as any Christian minister does, and the worshippers do not cover their heads. (It should be born in mind that Hebrew is the language of ancient Israel, in which the Old Testament was written, and as a language it has been resurrected to become the national tongue of the Republic of Israel. Jews from eastern Europe had a dialect language of their own, called Yiddish. This is not the language of the Jewish people but a peculiar form of German developed by the Jews of Germany, Poland, Russia and the Balkans. It is in the process of disappearing.)

Concerning God the Reformed have little to say. They are roughly in the same position as the Christian Unitarians. There is indeed one God but we really don't know much about him. The Scriptures should not be taken literally, and they should be interpreted in the light of modern science and sociology. The Talmud is not normative. Except for a warm attachment to the Jewish religious past the Reformed are the least Jewish of all believing Jews.

The third group in American Judaism forms the *Conservative* congregations. The Conservatives agree with the Orthodox on principle. They hold the Scriptures as indicative of right Jewish belief and they must be understood in the traditional sense. The Talmud also is to some degree normative. Conservatives, therefore, on principle keep the dietary laws and the ancient customs. But they also agree with the Reformed that Jewish faith must be adapted to the conditions of the time. They merely insist that this be done not according to the whims of each individual but by a responsible authority within the community and only after study and common deliberation.

Hence in worship services the Conservatives will use both English and Hebrew. Though they teach that Jews should eat only kosher food, yet they will permit necessary deviations from the traditional practices. On principle they will circumcise Jewish boys. The Conservatives also are more aware of the meaning of God than the Reformed. On the nature of Messiah they are as varied as the current Orthodox.

This group mediates between Orthodox and Reform. The Reformed have rejected any notion of the supernatural. The Orthodox do not theologize about the supernatural but the climate of their lives is supernaturally saturated. The Conservative consciously develop the notion of the supernatural, though they will not use the word.

There are other minor divisions within American Jewish religion. One of them is picturesque. These are the *Hasidim*. In centers where there is a sizeable Jewish community, the Hasidim (meaning the men of piety) are highly visible. They wear long black coats, wide-brimmed, round-crowned hats. They are all bearded and have curly sideburns. Often they wear no ties. They are not, as some people think, rabbis. They are Hasidim, a sect which was once quite numerous but is today diminishing in numbers. In matters of custom they are quite conservative and keep themselves separated from the prevailing cultures. They observe the dietary laws and Sabbath very strictly. They are simple people who, unlike the Orthodox, are not concerned with scholarship. They attach themselves to some rabbi who is their guide and leader in all things. With enthusiasm and joy, rather than with severity and formalism, they serve the Lord

who is very near to them always. They can live only in a
tightly connected community and they do not thrive in dis-
persion.

32. CO-OPERATIVE ORGANIZATIONS

The multitude of American churches in general, and within
Protestantism in particular, has made it desirable to found
interdenominational institutions which can realize projects
which are common to many churches. Because the goals are
common, they permit the collaboration of different churches,
and the combined action of all or many is more effective than
the efforts of only one group. Many of these united actions are
strictly practical and inspired by no other motive than to get a
worthwhile job done. Others, however, have a deeper inspiration. They desire that the churches become in some future day
organically and visibly one. Institutions and activities created
by this hope are called *ecumenical.* In this context the word
ecumenical means any effort to bring all the Christian Churches
together in the hope of having them ultimately become a single,
visible church. In such an enterprise the immediate goal of
action is not the only attraction for the collaborators. They look
for the fulfillment of their total hope in something which lies
far beyond the immediate objective of their endeavors.

In the United States there are interdenominational organizations of both kinds. Some are ecumenical and some are
merely, or at least mainly, practical.

The great ecumenical association is the *World Council of
Churches* (WCC). This federation is made up of some one
hundred and eighty churches of the whole world. Some Eastern
churches are members. The Catholic Church does not belong
to the Council. Most of the member churches are of the
Protestant tradition. The Council's central headquarters are in

Geneva but there is an office for the United States Conference of the World Council in New York City. The Council was born in 1948 in its first general assembly at Amsterdam, Holland. The second assembly was held in Evanston, Illinois, in 1954. The third assembly will take place in New Delhi in 1961. Between the sessions of the general assemblies standing committees meet at appointed times to carry on the ecumenical work of the Council, and a permanent secretariat is always at work. This association is certainly the most impressive interdenominational activity in our time. Its zeal and goal are worthy of admiration.

The *National Council of Churches of Christ in the United States of America,* usually called simply the National Council of Churches, was born as a practical union of American churches. It took its present form in 1950 after the foundation of the World Council of Churches with which the National Council works in close co-operation. The National Council was a merger of a number of earlier interdenominational organizations of which the most important was the *Federal Council of Churches of Christ in America* which had existed as a co-operative agency of twenty-six member churches. The present National Council is the expanded successor of the former organization. It is made up of thirty-four churches, all existing in the United States, most of which are Protestant. Its headquarters are in New York City and its directive authority lies in the triennial General Assembly. (The last meeting was held in the month of December of 1960 in San Francisco.) A standing General Secretariat carries on the work of the Council. Through its member churches the Council represents some 40,000,000 Christians and it works to give the practical witness of the federated churches to Christ by public action and word. Its commissions and divisions engage in a wide variety of programs: education, welfare, missionary work, etc.

The National Conference of Christians and Jews is not a federation of churches but an organized group of individuals striving to promote better understanding and friendly relations between the various religious communities in the United States. It is a corporation with its headquarters in New York City. It is not so much a religious union as a civic means to facilitate the co-operation and mutual understanding of Christian and Jewish citizens in America. The Conference engages in study, publishing study findings, and organizing meetings in different cities of the land.

YMCA and *YWCA*. The Young Men's Christian Association (or "Y") and the Young Women's Christian Association are worldwide unions with flourishing branches in the United States.

In 1844 a young Englishman, George Williams, a member of the Anglican church, was acutely conscious of the religious difficulties which faced the young Christian men employed in commerce and industry. He headed a small group of companions which founded the Young Men's Christian Association. The purpose of the society was to provide meeting places for young men where religion could be cultivated and friendship could be developed in a Christian atmosphere. The movement spread all over England and reached North America in 1851. The religion represented by the Y was evangelical Protestantism with no denominational identification. Yet the Y was not and is not a Protestant church, though its basic interests still remain evangelical.

The activities of the Y became many. All are directed to the formation of character in young men through group activity. Today the Y is highly visible because of the recreational programs it sponsors and directs. Y centers can be found in every city and large town. Many of the centers offer hotel facilities for men at a modest price. The centers also contain gymnasia, swimming pools, billiard parlors, bowling alleys, etc. They possess libraries and sponsor formal and informal educational courses. Lectures are also arranged. Religious services of a Protestant evangelical kind are conducted, the local lay secretary usually officiating. In the beginnings membership was open only to Protestants. Today it is open to all, but the general atmosphere is still mildly Protestant.

The Y offered its services to the armed troops in the last three wars. It also has its centers in universities, colleges and high schools. Similarly, Y centers are erected in railroad and industrial areas. The Association Press, a large publishing house, is also a project of the Y and the Press issues religious and educational books of popular appeal at low prices.

The world membership of the Y includes about 4,000,000 young men and the work reaches millions who are not members. In North America alone there are about 2000 centers with some 2,500,000 members. The American headquarters are in New York City.

The Young Women's Christian Association or YWCA is the feminine counterpart of the YMCA, though the two societies are not united. The YWCA is the result of the action of two Englishwomen, Miss Emma Roberts and Lady Kinnaird. In 1855 each began a society in England for young women in business and commerce; the first formed a prayer union and the second founded institutions and residences and programs of entertainment and fellowship for young women in a Christian environment. The two societies merged in 1887. The work parallels the activity of the YMCA in as far as it is adaptable to women. The YWCA has a much smaller membership, including some 500,000 in the whole world. The organization has been in the United States since 1858. The American headquarters are in New York City.

The American Bible Society is an association supported by many Protestant churches in this country. It is similar to such societies which can be found in England, Germany and other countries. The American society was started in 1816. The function of the Society is to facilitate the distribution of Bibles everywhere. For this purpose the Society buys Bibles from different publishing houses. For languages in which the Bible is not available the Society translates and prints it. The Society works without financial profit and sells its Bibles at cost or below cost. Translations are of great interest to the Society and it distributes the Scriptures in more than 200 languages. All its editions are well printed and attractively presented. The low cost makes them popular. In general the Bibles distributed are Protestant versions and the Society is a Protestant endeavor. Its headquarters are in New York City.

A Bible society with different aims than the American Bible Society is *The Gideons* whose legal title is the Christian Commercial Men's Association, International. It was founded in 1899 at Janesville, Wisconsin, but started its Bible work in 1908. The society is supported by free-will gifts and is not attached to any church or denomination. The founders, who were three travelling salesmen, realized that the presence of the Bible in lodgings for travellers could be a spiritual aid and consolation. In consequence, they distributed Bibles to hotels so that each room might have one. Today the society makes Bibles available to hotels, motels, Pullman cars, aeroplanes, schools, hospitals, jails. Gideons have also distributed Bibles to the armed forces. The distribution is free and in fifty years the Gideons have given away almost 3,000,000 Bibles. The Bibles are in English and the Gideons have a Protestant version printed for themselves in vast quantities. The title page will bear the Gideon symbol, an ancient Hebrew water pitcher with a handle on each side. This alludes to the Gideon story in the book of Judges (chap. vii). The Gideons distribute their Bibles in the United States, Canada and the East.

There are other interdenominational organizations but none as conspicuous as the ones here mentioned.

CHURCHES IN NORTH AMERICA

A FINAL WORD

We have now come to the end of this survey of the non-Roman churches in North America. It was of course impossible to describe in detail each of the more than two hundred and fifty churches into which modern men have become separated. But it may be helpful if some of the elementary and essential facts of our neighbors' religious views are at least partially known and understood.

Today there is a strong movement towards union among Protestant Christians. In the preceding chapters I have indicated where churches have come together, where they seem likely to, and where it is possible that they may in the future. This trend towards unity in one visible church, when it is consciously and formally advocated, goes by the name of the Ecumenical Movement. It is a vital and effective movement within Protestantism, largely spurred on by the World Council of Churches.

It is true that the fear, distrust and suspicion which for so long characterized relations between Christians of various confessions have, in recent times, greatly abated — at least on the theologian's level. But a sympathetic knowledge and understanding among *all* Christians is the first requisite of any ecumenic endeavor — namely, the endeavor to unite the churches to whatever degree is possible at a given moment. It may well be that the immediate task at hand for all Christians is to develop an ecumenical atmosphere — an environment not inimical to friendly and reasonable intercourse and discussion. There is a good deal to be done on this para- or pre-ecumenical level. It is to foster this developing action in the current scene that I have written this book.

INDEX

Index

Date Due

NOV 9 '73			
APR 8 '80			

Lincoln Christian College

Demco 38-297